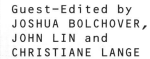

Guest-Edited by
JOSHUA BOLCHOVER,
JOHN LIN and
CHRISTIANE LANGE

DESIGNING THE RURAL

A Global Countryside in Flux

ARCHITECTURAL DESIGN
July/August 2016

Profile
No 242

About the
Guest-Editors

Joshua Bolchover,
John Lin and
Christiane Lange

05

Introduction
Where is the
Rural in an
Urban World?

Joshua Bolchover, John Lin
and Christiane Lange

06

Inventing
the Rural

A Brief History of
Modern Architecture
in the Countryside

Cole Roskam

14

Settling the
Nomads

Rural Urban Framework, an
Incremental Urban Strategy
for Ulaanbaatar, Mongolia

Joshua Bolchover

20

Rural Urban Framework (RUF),
Smart Collection Point,
Chingeltei, Ulaanbaatar,
Mongolia, 2015

Indefinitely
Intermediate

Processes of Ruralisation
in Chisinau, Moldova

Sandra Parvu

28

Cultivating the
Field in the
Global Hinterland

Community Building
for Mass Housing in the
Amazon Region

Rainer Hehl

34

Palm Oil

A New Ethics of
Visibility for the
Production Landscape

Milica Topalovic

42

Notes on Villages
as a Global
Condition

David Grahame Shane

48

Fieldoffice
Architects,
Jin-Mei
Parasitic
Pathway, Yilan
City, Taiwan,
2008

Fieldoffice
Architects
In Situ

Reflecting on the Rural–
Urban Mix in Yilan, Taiwan

Sheng-Yuan Huang
and Yu-Hsiang Hung

58

In the Hands
of the People

Harnessing the
Collective Power of
Village Life in India

Sandeep Virmani

66

ISSN 0003-8504
ISBN 978-1118-951057

Designing for an Uncertain Future

Rural Urban Framework, Shichuang Village House Prototype, Guangdong Province, China

John Lin

72

The Hunstad Code

Rules for the Planning of a Rural Town

Anders Abraham and Christina Capetillo

78

Anders Abraham and Christina Capetillo, Hunstad, Sweden, 2008-11

The Villages, Florida

Small-town Metropolitanism and the 'Middle of Nowhere'

Deane Simpson

86

New Territories

Deconstructing and Constructing Countryside – The Great Divide of Rural and Urban in Hong Kong

Christiane Lange

92

The Toshka Project

Colossal Water Infrastructures, Biopolitics and Territory in Egypt

Charlotte Malterre-Barthes

98

Best of Both Worlds

Lamenting Our Path to the Future

Stephan Petermann

106

Division: Yuen Long, New Territories, Hong Kong, 2014

Durana, Albania

A Field of Possibilities

Ambra Fabi and Giovanni Piovene

114

The Hinterland, Urbanised?

Neil Brenner

118

Counterpoint
Don't Waste Your Time in the Countryside

Patrik Schumacher

128

Contributors

134

Editorial Offices
John Wiley & Sons
25 John Street
London WC1N 2BS
UK

T +44 (0)20 8326 3800

Consultant Editor
Helen Castle

Managing Editor
Caroline Ellerby
Caroline Ellerby Publishing

Freelance Contributing Editor
Abigail Grater

Publisher
Paul Sayer

Art Direction + Design
CHK Design:
Christian Küsters
Christos Kontogeorgos

Production Editor
Elizabeth Gongde

Prepress
Artmedia, London

Printed in Italy by Printer
Trento Srl

Front cover: Rural Urban Framework (RUF), Mulan School and Educational Landscape, Guangdong Province, China, 2012. © RUF

Back cover: Rural Urban Framework (RUF), Taiping Bridge renovation, Guizhou Province, China, 2009. © RUF

Inside front cover: BAÚ Collaborative, workshop, Eden project, Bairro dos Mineiros, Parauapebas, Brazil, 2015– © Merle Sudbrock

04/2016

△D ARCHITECTURAL DESIGN

July/August	Profile No.
2016	**242**

Journal Customer Services
For ordering information, claims and any enquiry concerning your journal subscription please go to www.wileycustomerhelp.com/ask or contact your nearest office.

Americas
E: cs-journals@wiley.com
T: +1 781 388 8598 or
+1 800 835 6770 (toll-free in the USA & Canada)

Europe, Middle East and Africa
E: cs-journals@wiley.com
T: +44 (0) 1865 778315

Asia Pacific
E: cs-journals@wiley.com
T: +65 6511 8000

Japan (for Japanese-speaking support)
E: cs-japan@wiley.com
T: +65 6511 8010 or 005 316 50 480 (toll-free)

Visit our Online Customer Help available in 7 languages at www.wileycustomerhelp.com/ask

Print ISSN: 0003-8504
Online ISSN: 1554-2769

Prices are for six issues and include postage and handling charges. Individual-rate subscriptions must be paid by personal cheque or credit card. Individual-rate subscriptions may not be resold or used as library copies.

All prices are subject to change without notice.

Identification Statement
Periodicals Postage paid at Rahway, NJ 07065. Air freight and mailing in the USA by Mercury Media Processing, 1850 Elizabeth Avenue, Suite C, Rahway, NJ 07065, USA.

USA Postmaster
Please send address changes to *Architectural Design,* c/o Mercury Media Processing, 1634 E. Elizabeth Avenue, Linden, NJ 07036, USA.

Rights and Permissions
Requests to the Publisher should be addressed to:
Permissions Department
John Wiley & Sons Ltd
The Atrium
Southern Gate
Chichester
West Sussex PO19 8SQ
UK

F: +44 (0) 1243 770 620
E: Permissions@wiley.com

Subscribe to △D
△D is published bimonthly and is available to purchase on both a subscription basis and as individual volumes at the following prices.

Prices
Individual copies:
£24.99 / US$39.95
Individual issues on △D App for iPad:
£9.99 / US$13.99
Mailing fees for print may apply

Annual Subscription Rates
Student: £75 / US$117 print only
Personal: £120 / US$189 print and iPad access
Institutional: £212 / US$398 print or online
Institutional: £244 / US$457 combined print and online
6-issue subscription on △D App for iPad: £44.99 / US$64.99

Guest-Editors Joshua Bolchover and John Lin of Rural Urban Framework (RUF), and Christiane Lange, are colleagues at the University of Hong Kong. Combining research, projects and teaching, they are interested in the fate of rural territories across the globe, and how the urban future might be intertwined with the rural.

Soon after the announcement in 2005 by the Chinese government that its 11th Five-Year Plan would shift its focus towards constructing a 'new socialist countryside', RUF began working in various rural villages throughout China. Its built projects are a response to the processes of rural urbanisation. Recent work has included investigations of the impact of rural migration on the city fabric of Ulaanbaatar, Mongolia.

Christiane Lange has collaborated with RUF since 2008, for example on an exhibition within the Hong Kong Pavilion at the Venice Biennale (2010), where building projects were set against a panorama of rural-to-urban transformation. Identifying new forms of rural transformation has led to her current research on the city of Hong Kong and its hinterlands. Together with RUF, she co-edited the book *Homecoming: Materializing, Contextualizing and Practicing the Rural in China* (Gestalten, 2013), which gathers together the work of historians, theorists, educators and practitioners to discuss the role of the rural in Chinese development over the past 30 years.

RUF is a research and design laboratory within the Faculty of Architecture at the University of Hong Kong. Conducted as a non-profit organisation providing design services to charities and NGOs, it has now constructed over 15 projects in China and Mongolia, including schools, community centres, hospitals, village houses and bridges, as well as developing incremental planning strategies. As a result of this active engagement, RUF has been able to research the links between social, economic and political processes and the physical transformation of each village. The projects integrate local and traditional construction practices with contemporary technologies.

The recipient of numerous international awards including the Curry Stone Design Prize in 2015 and the Ralph Erskine 100 Years Anniversary Award 2014, given for innovation in architecture that 'primarily benefits the less privileged in society', RUF's research and built work has recently been published in the book *Rural Urban Framework: Transforming the Chinese Countryside* (Birkhäuser, 2013), which discusses not only its successful projects, but also the failures from which much can be learnt for the future.

INTRODUCTION

JOSHUA BOLCHOVER, JOHN LIN
AND CHRISTIANE LANGE

OMA,
The Interlace,
Singapore,
2013

Known as the 'vertical village',
this high-density private
residential development is an
idealisation of the rural as a
design concept and branding
strategy for urban housing.

Where is the Rural in an Urban World?

If the 20th century represented the rise of the megalopolis, could the 21st century mark a return to the countryside? Reacting to the flaunted statistic of living in an urbanised world, architects and urban thinkers are increasingly turning their attention to the rural. This territory has gained relevance beyond being a counterpoint to the urban; it is an emergent condition for innovation and exploratory research. This shift in focus underpins a fundamental question: How do we redefine the rural in a globalised urban world?

This issue of $\triangle$ tackles this subject by looking at different geographical sites where the very identity of the rural is being challenged and upended. It also brings together architects who have chosen to work in these locations, demonstrating how their approach to design practice has altered in response to the issues they have needed to address. The diversity of conditions outside the city has led to an equally distinct set of strategies and approaches.

We remain fascinated with the productive tension between the rural and urban. This threshold, on the edge of a transformation process, reveals the raw and immediate processes of urbanisation. This is not simply a question of the urban supplanting the rural; rather, the uniqueness of the rural, in terms of its social, political and economic make-up, changes and shapes how transformation takes place. The rural is the frontline of the urbanisation process.

The architects and theorists in this issue are not just rural practitioners; they are urbanists and urban architects, and through their work we can begin to understand how the dynamic conditions of the rural impact the future of our urbanised world.

The Global Rural

Depending on where you are in the world today, the rural has very different attributes. In developing countries it is volatile and full of contradictions: legally designated rural areas look like dense slums; factories intersect fields and farmers no longer farm. In contrast, in developed countries the rural has become a highly controlled landscape of production and consumption, in some cases a leisure landscape for tourism, retirement, second homes or recreation. This contrast reveals the rural to be an emerging territory that requires as much innovation, strategic thinking and design experimentation as the city.

Designing within this shifting context challenges the role of architects, their actions and their methods. Some architects still claim the rural as a site of authenticity – as protected enclaves preserving traditional livelihoods, craft techniques and construction methods. Vernacular rural architecture is often considered to be the originator of truth and beauty, an ingenious exchange between craftsman, climate and local knowledge. Yet the vernacular that seemingly dominates the contemporary rural landscape of developing countries is quite the opposite: generic concrete-framed structures, driven by economic need and oblivious to any contextual factors. In this regard, the rural is not a pastoral 'other' to the city; it too has become sullied and tainted by human occupation, often more dense, brutal and confrontational than the city itself. The same can be said of the rural in developed countries, where vernacular architecture manifests a form of exaggerated culture, catering to the tastes and expectations of urban tourists.

Designing the Rural explores the stark differences between the developing and developed world. The specific conditions of these rural territories are described alongside projects that work within these diversified conditions, producing architectural insertions, collective actions or new strategies. Rather than portray beautiful architecture in bucolic settings, the focus is on sites where their rural identity is being challenged. The issue investigates how architects and researchers have responded to these evolving conditions and are re-engaging with the rural as an experimental field of exploration.

Rural Urban Framework

The concept for the issue emerged from the work of Rural Urban Framework (RUF), a research and design collaboration based at the University of Hong Kong under the directorship of Joshua Bolchover and John Lin, with Christiane Lange as a longstanding collaborator. Our approach, which is mirrored in the content of the issue, is a dialogue between practice and research. RUF's design projects in rural China have demanded research into the larger stories impacting these sites. It became apparent that the era of economic reform under the Deng Xiaoping Communist Party beginning in the late 1970s had enabled the gradual dependency on and interconnection between rural and urban processes despite their continued political and social separation. The sites of RUF's projects evidence what Neil Brenner (in his article on pp 118–27) describes

'Hallstatt' village development, Boluo Township, Huizhou City, Guangdong Province, China, 2012

Replica of the Austrian alpine village of Hallstatt – the idealisation of a European rural condition transplanted in China.

Nomadic Green, Prinzessinnengarten (Princess Gardens), Moritzplatz, Kreuzberg, Berlin, 2009

The urban neighbourhood farm – a rural programme migrating to the urban.

Dug-out village, Shanxi Province, China, 2013

Rapid rural development is showcasing the collision of traditional vernacular forms and generic urban construction.

as the projection of urban processes of capital accumulation into rural areas. We became interested in recording the spatial characteristics of these flows as they touched the ground. The consequential landscape was full of contradictions and incoherencies: villages with diminishing populations building new houses; contested sites where rapid new development bordered ruinous and incomplete construction projects; new suburban enclaves in the midst of working farmland; and rural villages with populations and densities more attributable to urban areas. These paradoxes and disruptions challenged the notion of a seamless transition from the urban to the rural. Each aberration played witness to a complex interaction between rural and urban forces.

RUF's work operates in the hinterlands and peripheral rural areas where the effects of urbanisation are beginning to take hold. Some of our projects address gaps in this process. Infrastructure is often a key driver of urbanisation, facilitating the movement of goods, raw materials and labour; however, it can also disrupt more local forms of connection, bisecting farmland and dividing villages. At Lingzidi Village in Shanxi Province, the construction of both a highway and an elevated high-speed railway resulted in the destruction of several small bridges in the district that were vital connectors allowing produce from farmland to be collected and distributed to markets. Without them, the basic economy of the village went into decline. RUF's design for a new bridge (Lingzidi Bridge, 2012) reconnected this network and also defined a new social space within the village.

In the Mulan Primary School and Educational Landscape Project in Guangdong Province (2012 and 2014), the repository of earth created by the incision of the high-speed rail linking Guangzhou to Guilin had created an unstable mound on the site of the existing school. Rather than remove this slope or encase it in concrete, RUF saw this as an opportunity to define a programmatic landscape. Through reforming and manipulating the earth we created a reed-bed filtration system for a new toilet block that acted as a retaining wall framing a basketball court.

Both of the above projects demonstrate the need to consider the increasing number of sites that become disconnected or disrupted through infrastructural development. Although macro-infrastructure prioritises the co-option of rural territory for urban processes, tactical insertions of micro-infrastructures can facilitate local connectivity and begin to reconcile fragmented landscapes.

Other RUF projects embrace the contrasting speeds of rural development. At the Yongxin Secondary

Rural Urban Framework (RUF), Angdong Health Centre, Angdong Village, Hunan Province, China, 2015

RUF has created new rural institutions as part of the urbanisation process. This health centre was one of the first free rural hospitals in China.

Rural Urban Framework (RUF), House For All Seasons, Shijia Village, Shanxi Province, China, 2012

In the design of a single village house prototype, RUF attempted to combine the intelligence of traditional building methods with contemporary uses.

Rural Urban Framework (RUF), Lingzidi Bridge, Lingzidi Village, Shanxi Province, China, 2012

The construction of both a highway and an elevated high-speed railway resulted in the destruction of hundreds of small pedestrian bridges in the county. By rebuilding these links, RUF also had the opportunity to implement small-scale public spaces such as areas for washing clothes, fishing and resting.

RUF's work in rural China demonstrates an approach that is not contingent on scale or permanence; it is likely that many of our projects will not survive the pressures of urbanisation exerted upon them.

Rural Urban Framework (RUF), Yongxin Secondary School, Yongxin Town, Jiangxi Province, China, 2012

Embracing the speed and unpredictability of the urbanisation process, this school design prototype can be implemented in either rural or urban contexts.

Rural Urban Framework (RUF), Qinmo Community Centre, Qinmo Village, Guangdong Province, China, 2009

Working within and resisting the rapid speed of development endemic to rural China, the Qinmo Village project has embraced incremental planning by carefully implementing a series of small interventions such as this community centre, a library, primary school and public spaces as part of the transformation of the entire village.

School in Jiangxi Province (2012), the project was conceived as the anchor of the development of a new town on a greenfield rural site. The school itself had roughly the same number of inhabitants – around 2,000 – as Mulan village. Our strategy engaged with the unpredictability of the urbanisation process in the design of a walled enclosure that preserves the inner, collective life of the school despite possible future changes to its context. Conversely, at Qinmo Village in Guangdong Province we deployed a series of tactical insertions, including a community centre (2009), over nearly a decade to improve educational and public spaces.

RUF's work in rural China demonstrates an approach that is not contingent on scale or permanence; it is likely that many of our projects will not survive the pressures of urbanisation exerted upon them. Yet each asserts that the act of making architecture impacts the urban, that urbanism itself has no scale, and that each project is a result of a constant and evolving dialogue with its context. Moreover, there is no delineation between research and design – realising a project itself creates questions. Construction is only the beginning of testing our hypotheses as to how the project and its context will evolve.

Having worked primarily in China's hinterlands, we were curious to find out how other architects and theorists were approaching the problem of rural transformation in other locations. This issue of ⟁ brings together some of the emerging ideas and strategies for a global countryside in flux.

The Real and Imagined Rural

The issue opens with Cole Roskam's article 'Inventing the Rural' (pp 14–19), which reflects on the history of modern architecture with respect to the rural, and looks at the critical question of awareness when tackling the countryside, not just as a landscape requiring urban order, but with approaches that engage in its logic and specificity. The main section is then organised in three parts: 'Transforming the Rural', 'Defining the Village' and 'Constructing the Countryside'.

The articles in the 'Transforming the Rural' section explore sites where the rural has been an active agent in the process of transformation. Examples include those that are being impacted by massive rural migration to the city, the interference of rural morphologies within urban contexts, territorial-scaled landscapes of production, and an examination of spaces that are neither rural nor urban, but perhaps in-between states in an ongoing process of change. In 'Settling the Nomads: Rural Urban Framework, an Incremental Urban Strategy for Ulaanbaatar, Mongolia' (pp 20–27), Joshua Bolchover explores the unique example of informal settlements in this independent nation and demonstrates two constructed design projects that grapple with the complexity of rural migration to the city. Sandra Parvu's case study 'Indefinitely Intermediate: Processes of Ruralisation in Chisinau, Moldova' (pp 28–33) describes the intelligence of rural knowledge and rural appropriation within a city located at a geopolitical buffer between Europe and Russia.

A much more violent transformation is occurring at the edge of the Amazon rainforest in Brazil where speculative mass housing is bereft of any communal infrastructure. In 'Cultivating the Field in the Global Hinterland' (pp 34–41), Rainer Hehl uncovers this problem and proposes participatory design methods to instill community building through new social and ecological infrastructures. Focusing on the ramifications of contemporary production landscapes and their representation, in 'Palm Oil: A New Ethics of Visibility for the Production Landscape' (pp 42-7) Milica Topalovic explores this territory in Singapore's hinterland with Malaysia.

The 'Defining the Village' section focuses on a diverse set of design approaches to sustain rural areas, to allow them to evolve rather than being subsumed by urbanisation. In this section, we consciously avoid beautiful buildings in villages, opting instead for strategies with the power to affect the scale of the entire village, addressing its society, livelihood or construction. The articles explore the idea of the village as an architectural (and archetypal) proposition. The section is prefaced by David Grahame Shane's 'Notes on Villages as a Global Condition' (pp 48–57), which traces the history of the village as a design project and ultimately its role in the process of city building. Sheng-Yuan Huang and Yu-Hsiang Hung's 'Fieldoffice Architects In Situ: Reflecting on the Rural–Urban Mix in Yilan, Taiwan' (pp 58–65) describes the work of a unique practice that for over 20 years has worked solely in a single rural county in Taiwan. As the area has rapidly urbanised, many recent projects have re-inserted rural qualities back into the urban. In northern India, Sandeep Virmani describes the work of the Hunnarshala Foundation in his article 'In the Hands of the People: Harnessing the Collective Power of Village Life in India' (pp 66–71). The Foundation works with rural artisans, not only rebuilding houses but focusing on the intangible aspects of rurality strengthened through the process of building rural communities. The village is defined by its rare social capital.

In 'Designing for an Uncertain Future' (pp 72–7), John Lin looks at a recent RUF housing project in Shichuang Village in southern China. Anticipating new government policy changes, RUF here designed a prototype as an

Urbanus, *Tulou* social housing, Guangzhou City, Guangdong Province, China, 2009

top: Urbanus's modern adaptation of the *tulou* (earthen building) – a traditional communal residence found in Fujian Province – brings this rural typology back into the fabric of the city in the form of new social housing.

Tulou vernacular rural housing, Fujian Province, China, 2012

bottom: The vernacular *tulou* was originally designed with a great earthen wall as a system of defence. However, this traditional form of collective housing is now being enveloped by a new urban fabric.

architectural proposition for the use of existing government subsidies, which led to a series of new scenarios for rural house construction enabling the future commercial development of the village. Finally, Anders Abraham and Christina Capetillo's 'The Hunstad Code: Rules for the Planning of a Rural Town' (pp 78–85) establishes a strategy for designing a village in Sweden by first establishing a new village code. The project goes beyond formal attributes, defining the village as a set of social and spatial relationships.

The final, 'Constructing the Countryside' section of the issue challenges our perception of the rural. Most of us have an image of particular scenery in mind when thinking about countryside. With the increasing role of global tourism and reconstruction projects, metropolitan outposts, or high-tech infrastructures and landscapes, the contributions here explore the differences between the identity and appearance of a contemporary countryside. By further exploring estranged enclaves, in 'The Villages, Florida: Small-town Metropolitanism and the 'Middle of Nowhere'' (pp 86–91), Deane Simpson investigates urban outposts in the rural that reconcile the familiarity of village life and countryside by inheriting the artificial simulation of a metropolitan condition. Reflecting on the future development and governance of the countryside, in 'New Territories: Deconstructing and Constructing the Countryside' (pp 92–7), Christiane Lange reminds us of the consequences of top-down planning and amplifying a strong divide between the rural and urban. Whereas in 'The Toshka Project: Colossal Water Infrastructures, Biopolitics and Territory in Egypt' (pp 98–105), Charlotte Malterre-Barthes explores a development in which the identity of the landscape is being used by the government as a political instrument.

In asking for the 'Best of Both Worlds: Lamenting Our Path to the Future' (pp 106–13), Stephan Petermann points out the effects of globalisation and mobilisation and thus the conflicts created by global foreign investors, developers and architects designing a global imaginary of the countryside within the local context. As a response to decentralisation and laissez-faire development, in 'Durana, Albania: A Field of Possibilities' (pp 114–17) Ambra Fabi and Giovanni Piovene suggest the articulation of a scenic countryside via the introduction of leisure infrastructures. Lastly, in a theoretical engagement entitled 'The Hinterland, Urbanised?' (pp 118–27), Neil Brenner calls for the recognition of the 'hypertrophic city' – a landscape that blurs the divide between rural and urban by recognising and developing other forms of urbanisation.

The Urban Future

In a globalised world, our urban centres are becoming much more uniform. We have similar shops, similar experiences. The unique identity of the city is eroded, and the notion of the rural has suddenly become a source of cultural authenticity. But there is a yawning gap between the idea and the reality. And meanwhile our cities continue to grow, surpassing 10 million, then 30 million, and a newly planned urban megalopolis of 130 million in Beijing, so that we begin to question the scale of our cities. This is what makes the village so tantalising an idea: the evocation of a different scale of living, a different way of living, one based on a sense of community. Even though technology enables multiple virtual communities, we still long for the social intimacy of neighbourhood against the backdrop of rapid gentrification. Perhaps in its most basic form, interest in the rural is about another scale of living that offers alternatives to questions of work and lifestyle. Though the notion of an agricultural basis for the village is rapidly disappearing throughout much of the world, the village concept remains potent. In fact, we no longer grasp what it has become. This territory contains urgent issues, emergent conditions and new ideas. Its study has the potential to inform the urban. We need to start actively engaging, researching and designing the rural in order to shape our collective urban future. ⌀

Text © 2016 John Wiley & Sons Ltd. Images: pp 6-7 © OMA; p 8(t) © Alex Hofford/Sinopix; p 8(c) © Marco Clausen / Prinzessinnengarten; p 8(b), 9-11, 12-13(b) © Rural Urban Framework; pp 12-13(t) © URBANUS, photo Shen Xiaoming

Inventing the Rural

A Brief History of Modern Architecture in the Countryside

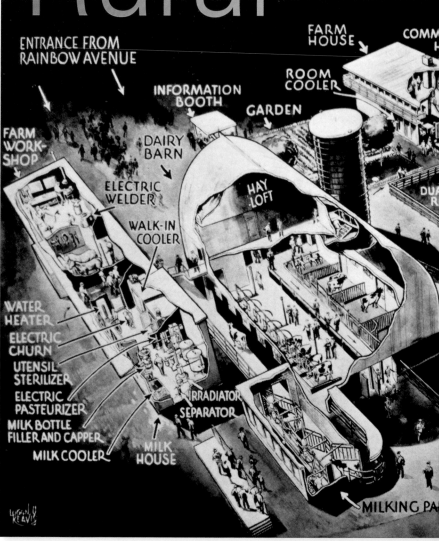

The rural has long occupied a valuable, if under-theorised position in modern architectural history. Here, **Cole Roskam**, Assistant Professor of Architectural History at the University of Hong Kong, highlights key moments in this history and, in doing so, illuminates a central paradox at the heart of architecture's various turns to the countryside; namely, can architects maintain the physical and social integrity of the rural when they are themselves a fundamental vector of its changing character?

Cole Roskam

REFRIGERATED STORAGE
FRUIT GRADER
CKING
GREEN-HOUSE
HOT BEDS
QUICK FREEZE
WATER WARMER
PUMP HOUSE
T RANGE POULTRY HOUSE
KITCHEN
BROODER HOUSE INCUBATOR
DISH WASHER
BATTERY LAYERS
OSAL
ATURE
TOR
SCALDER AND WAXER
WATER HEATER
EGG CLEANER AND CANDLER
SER
EAST ENTRANCE

THE ELECTRIFIED FARM
OF THE
ELECTRIC UTILITY INDUSTRY
NEW YORK WORLD'S FAIR
AN OPERATING FARM ONE ACRE
IN SIZE FEATURING MORE THAN
100 PRACTICAL APPLICATIONS
OF ELECTRICITY

Harrison & Fouilhoux

Electrified Farm

New York World's Fair

New York City

1939

The Electrified Farm was designed to demonstrate electricity's crucial role in liberating the American farmer from the constraints of traditional agricultural production while masking the transformative impact of such technology through a standard agricultural architectural vernacular.

The history of modern architecture is generally understood to be a history of the modern city. It was the unprecedented industrialisation of the early 20th-century metropolis, for example, that catalysed most of the interconnected groups broadly categorised as the Modern Movement in Europe, from Futurism to De Stijl, to the Congrès international d'architecture moderne (CIAM), among many others. Although Modernism is now understood as a broader, more geographically and culturally inclusive phenomenon shaped by a range of distinctive economic, political and social contexts beyond those existing in Europe, it is often against the backdrop of distinctly urbanised processes and environments that its origins, formations and physical production are still contextualised.[1] These alignments obscure the role played by urban's longtime Other, namely, the rural.

Architecture is a spatial practice; the rural is a spatial condition. Yet a cursory glance at the history of Modernism or contemporary architectural discourse suggests a distinct disciplinary bias towards urbanity, in all its meanings, as a prerequisite for critical consequential design. While the city continues to dominate our anxious and collective architectural imagination, the rural remains, as the British sociologist Howard Newby has argued, a frustratingly obfuscatory category to define in any discipline, let alone architecture.[2] Tremendous gaps and irregularities exist between particular intra-rural case studies; conversely, there are numerous intimate imbrications within many rural-urban environments that defy neat categorisation. The search for commonality and consistency in the rural is therefore difficult, leaving architects to engage with scales, systems and relationships from which they are often far removed, and which they are ill-equipped to address.

This essay reflects upon several basic dynamics at work in architecture's historical occupations with the rural at a time in which its elite, led by Rem Koolhaas, have discovered the countryside as a productive means of reinventing themselves and the discipline at large.[3] In fact, a closer look back through the modern history of architecture reveals numerous, often revitalising, engagements with the rural, particularly in the face of rapid and profound economic change. What might such recurrence reveal about the rural and its most recent identification as a potentially rich, if relatively fallow, physical and intellectual terrain for architecture today?

Cities in the Countryside

Efforts on the part of designers to extend some specific urban imaginary upon the rural date back at least to Andrea Palladio. Projects such as the Villa Rotonda (1571), illustrated here, famously inscribed a radical, more cultured aesthetic structure upon a rural environment perceived to be lacking in visual order. Palladio achieved a degree of aesthetic coordination – the reorganisation of individualised processes and parts into a cohesive visual and experiential whole – with the distinctive aesthetic pleasures of his urbane patrons in mind. The result, as the Venetian architect himself declared, were country houses best understood as 'little cities'.[4]

Palladio's work concretised a specific set of formal and programmatic fantasies that would persevere well into the 19th century. The notion that genteel architectural ideas derived from the city could simply be inserted into an unrefined rural condition, harmoniously or not, is evident in iconic examples ranging from Versailles (1623–82) to Monticello (1772), to Claude-Nicolas Ledoux's plan for the Royal Saltworks at Arc-et-Senans (begun 1775), among others. Each example positions the rural as an economically productive, if culturally barren landscape in need of refinement as well as supervision through more geometricised, and therefore more visibly laborious, physical form, including gardens, haciendas, palaces and plantations.

During the 19th century, important architectural reconceptualisations of the rural environment began to take shape. Rapid industrialisation prompted reconsideration of the countryside as more than a reservoir of natural resources or a theatrical backdrop for social signification, but as a vital antidote to the atmospheric and moral ills of urban life. Architects, planners and intellectuals retreated to the rural in search of some social and physical bulwark against the city's perceived civilisational decay. Charles Fourier, the French philosopher and socialist, famously rejected the commercial and industrial systems at work in the city in favour of what he saw as the potential for a new social organisation rooted in a form of communal agricultural production only possible in the countryside. Paradoxically, however, his imagined society's physical composition would be 'vastly different from those of our villages and towns, which are perversely organized and meant for families having no societary relations'.[5] Out of fear for the perceived 'chaos' and 'filth' of rural France, Fourier insisted upon the construction of a Phalanstery (1836), a massive physical extension of the very urban conditions it was designed to escape. The Phalanstery was imagined to comprise a central physical core featuring dining rooms, a library, meeting rooms and an observatory, while two flanking wings included workshops, ballrooms, larger meeting halls as well as apartments. Street galleries – an apparent transplantation of the Parisian Arcades to the countryside – snaked their way through the Phalanstery, where they provided space for circulation, social interaction and communication as well as a contained heated environment within which one could enjoy the theatre and opera 'without worrying about the mud and the cold'.[6]

Like its Palladian predecessors, the legacy of Fourier's utopian vision can be traced through a range of subsequent collective models, from New Harmony in Indiana to the socialist Chinese *danwei*, or workers' unit. These projects stitched particular sets of urban amenities into the pre-existing rural fabric, resulting in the perceived best of both possible 'worlds' – a rustic environment transformed through the rigours of urban design into something more aesthetically and socially legible. As ambitious architectural efforts in formal, programmatic and physical conflation, however, rural collectives often failed to recognise the pre-existing economic and social systems already at work within the countryside, or the speed with which urban industrialism had already begun to disrupt them. Nevertheless, they envisioned a physical relationship between architecture and landscape that expressed new technological, economic and social ideals – an important ideological antecedent to the Modern Movement itself.

Modernism's Architectural Pastoral

Frank Lloyd Wright's Broadacre City is perhaps the best-known example of the countryside's active, if under-theorised role in 20th-century architectural experimentation. First imagined in the late 1920s in response to Le Corbusier's Contemporary City proposal (1922), Broadacre City comprised an expandable, 4-square-mile (10-square-kilometre) plot of land that promised each resident at least one acre (0.4 hectare) to live on, ambitiously combining standardised single-family housing units with ample room for gardening and animal husbandry.[7] Although Wright initially devised the project to provide work for his Taliesin-based students, it nevertheless offered a distinctly American model of collective living balanced by equal parts self-sufficiency and communal living – a hypothetical 'Ruralism as distinguished from *Urbanisme*', declared Wright.[8]

Charles Fourier

Phalanstery

1836

Although Fourier argued that his Phalanstery did not bear any resemblance to a particular urban or rural architectural typology, the scale and complexity of the structure's programme gave it a distinctly urbanistic atmosphere.

L'AVENIR.

Perspective d'un Phalanstère ou Palais Sociétaire dédié à l'humanité.

Yet Le Corbusier harboured rural fantasies of his own. Over the course of the 1930s, and as Mary McLeod has previously discussed, Le Corbusier imagined two proposals, Ferme Radieuse (1933–4) and Village Radieux (1934–8), each of which were designed to maintain the family-run farm as the fundamental module of French agricultural production.[9] The Ferme Radieuse constituted a 20-hectare (50-acre) plot consisting of fields, a barnyard and the family home, each aligned along a central north–south service route. Village Radieux comprised a series of cooperative facilities, including a grain silo, grocery store and school, together with an apartment block and social club for workers as well as a town hall. Its asymmetrical east–west plan linked to a national highway with a half-cloverleaf intersection, and may be considered an important precursor to Le Corbusier's later work at Saint-Dié (1945) and Chandigarh (1951–65).[10]

In their respective architectural idealisations of the rural, both Wright and Le Corbusier responded to international economic crisis with distinctive collectivist sentiment that may champion a somewhat nostalgic perception of agrarian life, but may also be understood as an implicit critique of capitalism itself.[11] Each did so in contrasting ways. Le Corbusier's proposal, for example, industrialised the farm in an effort to ameliorate the class-based tensions at work between France's urban and rural populations. Wright, by contrast, offered a new spatial and organisational paradigm grounded in policy – an architectural system organised around cooperative social credit, and therefore designed to eliminate both rent and real-estate speculation.

Nor were Wright and Le Corbusier alone in positing the rural as new conceptual territory for architectural utopia. A series of model farm projects displayed at both the Chicago and New York World's Fairs in 1934 and 1939 respectively conveyed more commercially enterprising, but similarly opportunistic, visions of a new rural modernity. Here, companies such as General Electric and Firestone Tire and Rubber, working in conjunction with the US government's Rural Electrification Administration (REA), trumpeted electricity to promote new architectural systems built around industrial products ostensibly designed to save American farmers time as well as money. Although few farmers could realistically afford them, these goods dazzled the fair-going public.[12] They also remind us of modern architecture's active, if occasionally naive participation in the rural's rapid utilisation as a marketplace.

Only after the Second World War, and faced with the overwhelming opportunities and challenges presented by postwar reconstruction and international economic expansion over the course of the 1950s, did architects begin to come to terms with their unwitting role in commodifying the rural. Examples include Hassan Fathy's New Gourna project, initiated in 1945 and ultimately published more than 20 years later as *Gourna, A Tale of Two Villages* (1969) and *Architecture*

Andrea Palladio

Villa Rotonda

Vicenza

Italy

1571

below left: Palladio described the building as a theatre of nature, and a space from which the spectacle of the countryside could be enjoyed.

Frank Lloyd Wright

Broadacre City

1958

below: The architect considered the project to be uniquely American, rooted in self-sufficiency as well as the collective national spirit.

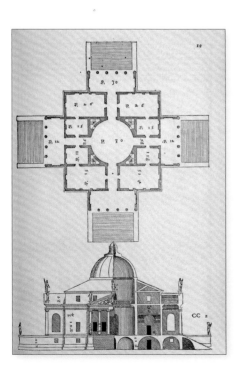

for the Poor (1973); Bernard Rudofsky's *Architecture Without Architects* (1964); and John FC Turner's *Housing By People: Towards Autonomy in Building Environments* (1976).[13] Each author responded to widening professional critique and disillusionment with radical reconceptualisations of the relationship between architecture and rural environments – efforts that sought to omit the architect from the equation altogether. These works may have positioned the vernacular as a source for architectural innovation, but in doing so they also relied upon the same paternalistic attitude towards the countryside and its building practices established centuries earlier – a landscape crafted anonymously and shaped by some intrinsic system of aesthetic and physical ordering to which, as seen in the case of New Gourna, the architect could somehow contribute in unobtrusive yet reaffirming ways.

Return to the Rural

For all of the inspired architectural work undertaken in rural contexts past and present, the practical and ideological promise of the city remains potent in many parts of the world. This is evidenced by, among other examples, China's ongoing efforts to relocate 250 million people to its cities in the name of furthering the country's economic transformation.[14] Not surprisingly, however, several members of China's architectural avant-garde, most notably Wang Shu, have reacted to China's rapid urbanisation by embracing the rural as their preferred site for practice. For growing numbers of architects all over the world, then, the countryside still beckons as a sanctuary from the city's economic and social abstractions.

For all of the inspired architectural work undertaken in rural contexts past and present, the practical and ideological promise of the city remains potent in many parts of the world.

Le Corbusier

Village Radieux

Piacé

France

1934–8

The clover-leaf ramp connecting the village to a national highway suggests Le Corbusier's commitment to dissolving the barriers between the rural and urban experience in France.

Ultimately, we may understand this most recent return of the professional architect to the rural as a signal of the discipline's ambivalence with capitalism and its insatiable globalising reach. The distinctive localities, particular logics and unique sets of problems at work in the rural present opportunities for an architecture that adapts to ecological change while accommodating geographic and cultural difference. If history provides any lessons for this most recent disciplinary fascination with the rural, however, it is that architects must reconcile their impulse to redefine and reimagine space with the understanding that they themselves constitute influential carriers of new practices, forms and tastes that automatically and inextricably transform what rurality looks like, where it exists and how it performs. The standard modes and means by which the discipline has historically participated within the rural no longer suffice. Architects need not frame the rural as a site requiring more urbane form and structure, but rather acquiesce to the reality that it is the urban that has always required the rural, which tirelessly and unsustainably supplies our industrialised landscapes with the food, water and energy they require to exist. Consequently, the rural should figure as an active and prominent agent in any collectivised effort on the part of the discipline to move beyond the techno-utopian fantasies of the past and present towards a more self-restrained grounded future. ⌂

Hassan Fathy

New Gourna masterplan

Egypt

1945

By insisting New Gourna residents adapt to a particular architectural aesthetic and planned village environment, Fathy failed to recognise the distinctive living patterns and preferences of Egyptian villagers eager to move beyond the constraints of the past.

1. See, for example, Le Corbusier, *The City of To-Morrow and Its Planning* [1929], Dover Publications (New York), 1987, and Gyan Prakash and Kevin M Kruse (eds), *The Spaces of the Modern City: Imaginaries, Politics and Everyday Life*, Princeton University Press (Princeton, NJ), 2008.
2. Howard Newby, 'Locality and Rurality: The Restructuring of Rural Social Relations', *Regional Studies*, 20 (3), 1986, pp 209–15.
3. 'Rem Koolhaas in the Country', *ICON*, 23 September 2014: www.iconeye.com/architecture/features/item/11031-rem-koolhaas-in-the-country.
4. Andrea Palladio, *The Four Books of Architecture* [1570], MIT Press (Cambridge, MA), 1997, p 46.
5. Jonathan Beecher and Richard Bienvenu (eds), *The Utopian Vision of Charles Fourier: Selected Texts on Work, Love, and Passionate Attraction*, Jonathan Cape (London), 1972, p 240.
6. *Ibid*, p 245.
7. Frank Lloyd Wright, 'Broadacre City: A New Community Plan', in Robert Twombly (ed), *Frank Lloyd Wright: Essential Texts*, WW Norton (New York) 2009, p 257. Originally published in *The Architectural Record*, 1935.
8. Cited in Neil Levine, *The Architecture of Frank Lloyd Wright*, Princeton University Press (Princeton, NJ), 1996, p 221.
9. Mary McLeod, 'Piacé: Ferme Radieuse and Village Radieux', in Jean-Louis Cohen (ed), *Le Corbusier: An Atlas of Modern Landscapes*, Museum of Modern Art (New York), 2013, pp 185–92.
10. *Ibid*, p 190.
11. Raymond Williams, *The Country and the City*, Hogarth Press (London), 1993, p 35.
12. Sarah Rovang, 'Envisioning the Future of Modern Farming: The Electrified Farm at the 1939 New York World's Fair', *Journal of the Society of Architectural Historians*, 74 (2), June 2015, pp 201–22.
13. Hassan Fathy, *Gourna, A Tale of Two Villages*, Ministry of Culture (Cairo), 1969, and *Architecture for the Poor: An Experiment in Rural Egypt*, University of Chicago Press (Chicago, IL), 1973; Bernard Rudofsky, *Architecture Without Architects*, Museum of Modern Art (New York), 1964; John FC Turner, *Housing By People: Towards Autonomy in Building Environments*, Marion Boyars (London), 1976.
14. Ian Johnson, 'Leaving the Land: China's Great Uprooting – Moving 250 Million Into Cities', *New York Times*, 15 June 2013: www.nytimes.com/2013/06/16/world/asia/chinas-great-uprooting-moving-250-million-into-cities.html?pagewanted=all.

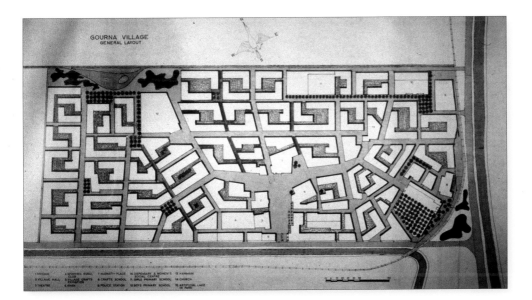

GOURNA VILLAGE
GENERAL LAYOUT

The rural should figure as an active and prominent agent in any collectivised effort on the part of the discipline to move beyond the techno-utopian fantasies

Settling

the

Rural Urban Framework (RUF),
Smart Collection Point,
Chingeltei,
Ulaanbaatar,
Mongolia,
2015

The prototype in November,
six months after completion.

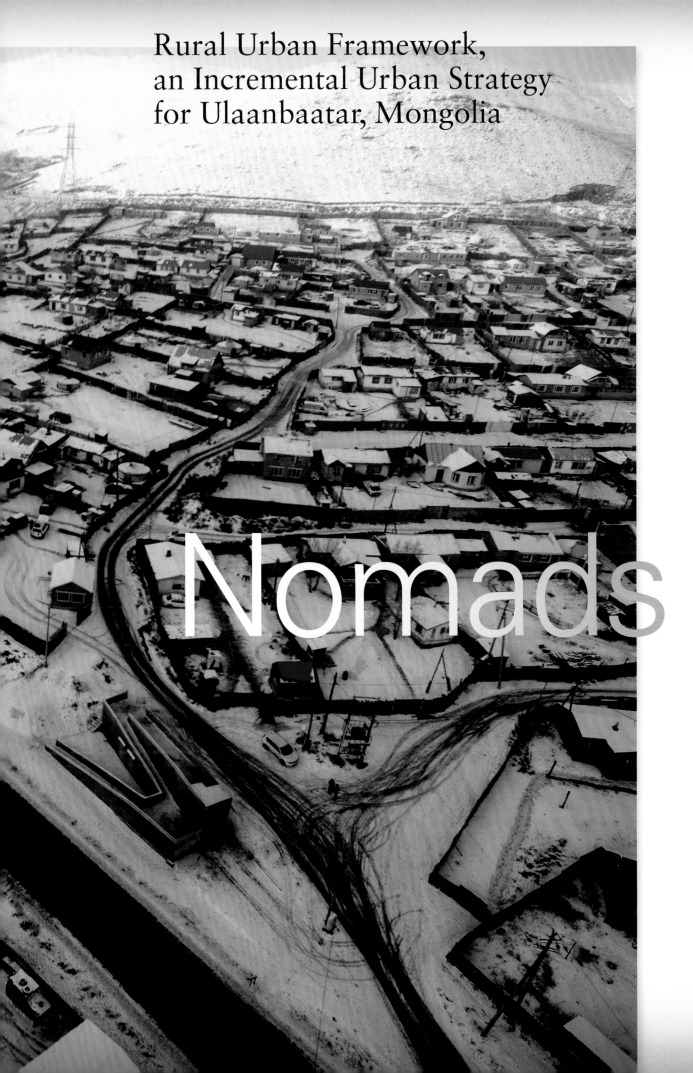

Rural Urban Framework,
an Incremental Urban Strategy
for Ulaanbaatar, Mongolia

Nomads

Over the last quarter-century, labour prospects linked to the discovery of exploitable natural resources have drawn former nomads to construct their traditional tent-houses in an ever-expanding, infrastructureless sprawl around the Mongolian capital. Guest-Editor **Joshua Bolchover** sets out how the collaborative practice Rural Urban Framework, which he co-founded, is engaged in establishing a strategy to solve the practical problems posed by this transition of nomadic structures to a sedentary setting.

A *ger* settlement at the fringe of Ulaanbaatar, Mongolia, February 2014

The most recent migrants settle at the periphery of the city.

Mongolia is facing a critical moment in its urban transformation. The country evolved from a period of economic hardship immediately following Soviet withdrawal in 1989, to a democratic electoral system and free-market economy. The discovery of vast reserves of coal, gold and copper, together with the promise of development projects, made the capital city – Ulaanbaatar – the focus of rural migration. The ensuing optimism that followed predicted GDP growth rates of 17 per cent in 2011, and led nomadic herdsmen to sell their livestock and move to the city in search of a better life. For many others, the extremely cold winter in 2010 killed their livestock, sealing their fate and leaving them little choice other than to move to the city. As a result, the population of Ulaanbaatar has doubled since 1989 and the city's territory has expanded from 130 square kilometres (50 square miles) to 4,700 square kilometres (1,800 square miles).[1]

The scale and speed of settlers has disrupted and pressurised the limited city resources, challenging employment, healthcare, education and other basic urban services. As this population has no prior experience of living among others – some state there is no word for 'community' in Mongolian – or in situ, in one home on a single plot of land, it is a unique and urgent situation. A diversity of issues – cultural, social, infrastructural and spatial – has arisen due to the contrast between nomadic, rural livelihoods and sedentary urban living. The situation is compounded by the local limits of the ground: arid soils, limited water and a harsh climate that sees temperatures plummet to negative double-digit figures between November and March.

Rural Urban Framework (RUF) began working in Ulaanbaatar in 2014. An initial exploratory trip led to a commission from the Asia Foundation to design and construct two waste-collection prototypes. RUF conceptualised these as activators of part of a larger incremental strategy to evolve the city's *ger* districts into a viable urban construct. The ongoing project illustrates how the rural has impacted the urban, the ineffectiveness of top-down planning models in this context, and RUF's position as an enabler, creating robust forms and constellations of programmes that can withstand and adapt to the pressures of transformation.

Zuun Ail *ger* district,
Ulaanbaatar,
Mongolia,
February 2014

Smoke billows from *ger* chimneys
in a dense, mid-tier district.

Becoming Urban

The nomads settle on any available land, occupying residual inner areas, slopes and the periphery of the city. When migrants arrive they erect a traditional felt tent – a *ger* – and surround the plot with a fence constructed from wooden posts or salvaged metal, often from discarded food or oil cans. This plot is called a *khashaa*: each new migrant, as a Mongolian national, has the right to stake a claim to own a land parcel of 700 square metres (7,535 square feet). The extent and rapidity of the growth of the *ger* settlements has meant that the provision of the most basic services of urban life has not been viable: water is fetched from kiosks; pit latrines are dug on site; and garbage goes uncollected. Coal smog hovers over the city during the winter as *ger* residents burn fuel to stay warm.

Each *khashaa* is inscribed with traces of the changes and adaptations that have occurred as each rural family has assimilated to urban life. Over time, they become a repository for both the resources and the detritus of everyday living. This changes according to the location of the plot. *Ger* districts are classified as central, mid and fringe sites. Each represents different settlement time periods with the most established closest to the city core and the most recent migrants settling at the edge of the city. Fringe districts such as Khan-Uul are more rural in character; within the *khashaa* here, cows and pigs are reared, vegetables are grown, and greenhouses are built. In Chingeltei district, a mid-*ger* area, plots tend to be smaller, sometimes on steep terrain, and are cluttered with heaps of rubber tyres, junk metal, bricks, sand or machinery parts, reflecting the shift to more urban economic activities. In both locations, some plots have more than one *ger*, either for children or to support family relatives who have just moved to the city. In others, people are transitioning from their *gers* into small houses: usually self-built, single-storey brick and timber constructions. The most basic house replicates the organisation of the *ger* as an open-planned room with no separating walls between different functions. As income improves, some residents build bigger two-storey houses with room divisions.

The ongoing project illustrates how the rural has impacted the urban, the ineffectiveness of top-down planning models in this context

Water kiosk,
Gandan district,
Ulaanbaatar,
Mongolia,
February 2014

Water is collected via kiosks that operate like petrol station pumps, and delivered via trucks or siphoned from underground aquifers.

The spectrum of different states of transformation of the *khashaa* reflects a process of assimilation from rural to urban and from nomadic to sedentary.[2] However, there is no concurrent upgrading of urban infrastructure or the provision of public buildings or spaces. The expansion of the city becomes an extreme form of informal suburbanisation. Unlike other informal settlements in developing countries, these districts are not illegal as each new migrant has the right to landownership. But they are still stigmatised as problem areas – effectively slums – that are seen as a hindrance to Ulaanbaatar's evolution into a 'modern' capital.

In response, the city is moving forward with radical redevelopment plans that include highways and roads, satellite towns, an airport, and the complete redevelopment of many *ger* districts, financed through the 2012 Chinggis Bond – a sovereign bond of US$1.5 billion – issued to sell its debt and raise capital with the primary objective to turn resources into hard cash through improved extraction, infrastructure and energy supply.[3] However, this bond will ultimately have to be paid back, creating a potentially vulnerable economy, highly susceptible to currency devaluation and the capriciousness of commodity prices. Despite improvements, particularly in local road infrastructure since 2012, the forecasted economic returns have not occurred owing to political stalemates with mining companies and the cost of extraction compared to the decreased value of commodities. As a result, development has stalled. Without investment, the wholesale redevelopment of *ger* districts has not been realisable. Given their scale and continued expansion within the city, this is unlikely ever to become a feasible solution. Meanwhile, the intrinsic problems directly related to nomadic structures becoming sedentary – the absence of sewage collection, water supply and solid waste – continue unabated.

Incremental Change

Rural Urban Framework's aim is to create a strategy for incremental change that can allow *ger* districts to evolve into viable settlements that are integrated into the future fabric of the city. Recognising that these settlements act as a critical hinge between the rural and urban – as a space of assimilation and adaptation and a vital exchange point between nomadic and settled forms of life – the intention is to seek to maintain their role, yet augment and enhance their process of transformation.

RUF began with the design of prototypes that focused on urgent issues such as housing, unemployment and the lack of infrastructure. Each was designed to allow for adaptation in anticipation of future changes to the context. As conceptual tools, prototypes help to link different programmes, inhabitants and stakeholders in order to stimulate economies and activities. For instance, the Linear Housing Prototype involves residents pooling their land to take a shareholding in the overall development with the main investor; while the Land-house is a ring of collective housing around a shared land resource that residents can use for agricultural production. Despite the increasing amount of construction occurring in the city, workers are poorly trained: the Materials Training Market prototype links a construction materials market with a vocational training centre to develop skill-based trades.

The Ger Housing Prototype strategically sets out a mechanism for the incremental transformation of the *khashaa* plot itself. The intention is to provide an off-grid infrastructure for water, sewage and heat supply that is embedded within the perimeter wall of

each plot. Different types of accommodation units can plug into this service wall, including the *ger*, a self-build house, or other typologies such as live-work units or vertical houses, allowing resident-owners to lease apartments to new migrant families. The infrastructural wall can connect to other plots, providing an armature enabling different speeds of development to occur. It enables each family to grow and change incrementally, facilitating opportunities for entrepreneurial activities such as shops, workspaces or rental units. This maintains the flexibility inherent in the *khashaa* itself, and the ability for it to accommodate different uses depending on whether the plot is situated in a central, mid or more rural district. Given the current financial impossibility to connect each *ger* district to a mains water and sewage system, the off-grid mechanism allows for smaller-scaled, autonomous systems to be implemented. In the future these can extend and link to other neighbourhoods and, should it become feasible in the long term, connect to a citywide infrastructural network.

The issue of solid waste collection is tackled through the concept of Intelligent Infrastructures – micro-insertions that link the daily routines of residents to waste and recycling facilities. The prototype addresses the immediate need to have somewhere to drop off rubbish, however the project is designed so that spaces within the structure can adapt into community facilities if and when metropolitan door-to-door waste collection is introduced.

Reality Check

Rural Urban Framework arrived at the city with a book of these prototype design ideas that were then shared and tested with potential stakeholders and experts including university professors, various NGOs, policy think-tanks, the planning department and the mayor's office. A meeting with the Asia Foundation, which was undertaking a project to investigate how solid waste collection in *ger* areas could be improved, was particularly fruitful. For rural nomads, waste in the form of plastic bottles, glass and cans is an unfamiliar urban phenomenon, and without clear systems of collection, garbage accumulates in gulleys, roadside verges and streams. The Foundation produced an interactive community map of *ger* districts from data gathered through numerous meetings with local residents that provides a database for local services such as bus stops, playgrounds, clinics, schools and water kiosks. It also shows areas of illegal dumpsites alongside official sites for waste collection. From this data, the Foundation was able to identify the worst areas for rubbish build-up alongside certain neighbourhoods, or *khoroos*, where it had forged good relationships with local leaders. RUF's brief was to create a demonstration project that could facilitate the hygienic collection of rubbish through Smart Collection Points. This involved RUF focusing on the architecture while the Asia Foundation was engaged in neighbourhood participation and outreach, improving the scheduling of trucks, and influencing mayoral policy on citywide waste collection. Based on the Foundation's site research, two locations were selected to implement and test the viability of RUF's prototype: one in the fringe district of Khan-Uul and the other in the mid-*ger* area of Chingeltei.

At Chingeltei, the site was located by the side of a recently constructed road on an uneven dirt slope. RUF's scheme took advantage of the height difference of the topography to form a ramp leading from the high ground to the road and bus stop with several places for rubbish drop-off along the way. A recycling station was contained under the ramp, which splayed apart to

Interior of a typical *ger*,
Ulaanbaatar,
Mongolia,
November 2015

The family moved to the city in 2000
from a rural village 1,000 kilometres
(620 miles) away. The father is an
ambulance driver.

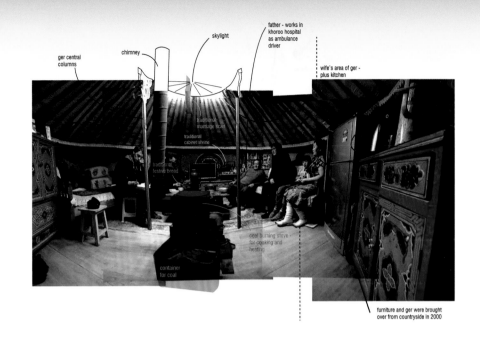

The issue of solid waste collection is tackled
through the concept of Intelligent Infrastructures
– micro-insertions that link the daily routines of
residents to waste and recycling facilities.

Khashaa plots at Chingeltei
and Khan-Uul,
Ulaanbaatar,
Mongolia,
November 2015

The traces of uses within each household
plot reflect the differences between more
rural or urban *khashaas*.

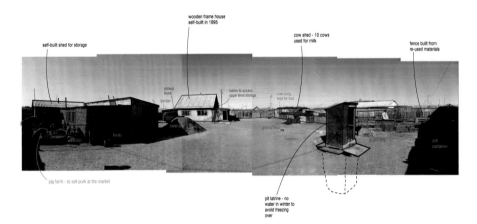

RUF here created an artificial topography by excavating 1.5 metres (5 feet) below ground for the collection, and plus 1.5 metres for the drop-off with a retaining wall holding this new mound in place.

Rural Urban Framework (RUF), Smart Collection Point, Chingeltei, Ulaanbaatar, Mongolia, 2015

top: The completed Smart Collection Point prototype at Chingeltei.

right: A local resident walks up the ramp to deposit her rubbish at the Smart Collection Point prototype.

create an open public space. At Khan-Uul, the primary issue on the flat terrain was how to ensure easy access for the public dropping off their trash as well as for the collectors. RUF here created an artificial topography by excavating 1.5 metres (5 feet) below ground for the collection, and plus 1.5 metres for the drop-off with a retaining wall holding this new mound in place.

Owing to the financial pressures of the timescale, the projects were built during harsh winter conditions, which meant that anti-freeze had to be included in the concrete to prevent the water content from freezing. On inspection in February 2015 it was still unclear whether the roof structure at Khan-Uul had in fact cured or was being held together with solid ice. However, in November that same year RUF arrived to discover a mound of rubble and a dead, frozen dog. It became apparent from the residents that the building had been demolished just a few days before, but it was unclear as to why.

Despite this huge disappointment, the very act of the roof's failure is evidence of the magnitude and complexity of the problem. It has opened up many more questions that demand investigation with respect to the management and operation of the prototype and lack of stakeholder buy-in. It has also forced a re-evaluation of RUF's strategies and a rethinking of how to build in the public realm. In order for the larger ambition of the project to be effective, this feedback loop needs to be taken on board to revise and alter the current design thinking.

RUF returned in February 2016 to initiate a new round of prototypes based on two updated tracks. The first represents the insertion of 'alien' forms: new compositions of programmes that address urgent issues that have arisen as a consequence of rural migration. The other sets out to evolve and complement the current process of rural-urban assimilation, to tweak and enhance everyday habits and to open up new opportunities for growth: for example, in relation to informal work or self-build houses. Strategically, RUF intends to build up a series of prototypes that act together to form more embedded urban organisations that can anchor the future growth of the community. Rather than erase the legacy of the nomadic rural culture with a standardised, generic urban form, incremental design enables more unique and adaptable models to emerge from the specific characteristics of the place.[4] ⌂

Notes
1. Takuya Kamata *et al*, *Mongolia: Enhancing Policies and Practices for Ger Area Development in Ulaanbaatar*, World Bank Publications (Herndon, VA), 2010.
2. Joel Eric Miller, 'Nomadic and Domestic: Dwelling on the Edge of Ulaanbaatar, Mongolia', PhD thesis, University of California, 2013.
3. Economic Research Institute, 'An Economic Impact Assessment of the Committed Chinggis Bond Allocation', December 2013: www.eri.mn/index.php/mn/component/content/article/94-research/204-2013-11-14-10-18-50.
4. The current research project 'Incremental Urbanism: Ulaanbaatar's Ger Settlements' is funded by the Research Grants Council of the Hong Kong Special Administrative Region.

Rural Urban Framework (RUF),
Smart Collection Point,
Chingeltei,
Ulaanbaatar,
Mongolia,
2015

The collection point in context showing the bus route and truck collection.

Rural Urban Framework (RUF),
Smart Collection Point,
Khan-Uul,
Ulaanbaatar,
Mongolia,
2015

The Khan-Uul prototype in the last stages of construction.

Strategically, RUF intends to build up a series of prototypes that act together to form more embedded urban organisations that can anchor the future growth of the community.

Courtyard,
68 Sciusev Street,
Chisinau,
Moldova,
2015

The additions to the main facade on the right, the fencing of the area in the background, as well as the vegetation modify the spatial experience to the extent that the lot is unrecognisable on the cadastral plan.

Processes of Ruralisation in Chisinau, Moldova

Indefin
Intermed

For a capital city, Chisinau displays an unusual proliferation of vernacular architecture – conceived in relation to the natural rather than political landscape. Architect, writer and educator **Sandra Parvu** examines how the Moldovan government's limited resources to impose urban order have allowed urban rurality to flourish, leading to a harmonious balance between the metropolitan and the pastoral.

Sandra Parvu

The last hours of 2011 were captured by the artist Pavel Braila and produced as a film entitled *New Year Dissection* (2012).[1] Three adjacent screens display festivities in the public and private spheres of Chisinau, the Moldovan capital. Children perform end-of-year spectacles, and shoppers cross open-air markets with displays of exotic fruit, champagne and Christmas decorations. At home, hands prepare traditional dishes, and televisions offer messages of happiness and success in the background. As night falls, an image of the triumphal arch in Chisinau shows two minutes to ten on the clock. The middle and right screens are images of the Kremlin broadcast by Russian television: it is two minutes to midnight on the Spasskaya watchtower. A few seconds later, the three screens make the situation explicit. As Moscow enters 2012, the Moldovan capital, although two hours behind, stands up to toast the New Year: fireworks explode, home videos show family members kissing and celebrating indoors. Two hours later, fireworks explode again, and other families are shown kissing and celebrating again. The film poignantly puts forth the rhythm of a city living in two different time zones: Moscow time, and its own time shared with Romania, Bulgaria and Greece.

To insist on the mutual exclusivity of separate time zones[2] seems irrelevant in a country that celebrates Christmas twice, according to the Julian and Gregorian calendars. This double dating results from a spatial condition in which borders have dramatically shifted 'as various powers exerting influence over the area have either expanded or contracted their spheres of influence'[3] and shaped the imaginary of its residents. First situated at the margins of the Russian and Ottoman empires, then a republic in the outer reaches of the Soviet Union, and today a small independent country acting as a buffer between European and Russian interests, Moldova is an 'institutionalised borderland, in the sense that it has always been located in a peripheral position with respect to centres of political, and often also economic power'.[4] It shares the condition of being a geopolitical in-between with neighbouring countries Romania and Bulgaria, as well as with the countries of the Balkan peninsula.[5]

Another layer added to the spatio-temporal in-between is the label 'transition country' since Moldova has travelled from a market to a planned economy and back. In a city where one can ask a question in Romanian and get an answer in Russian, it is not surprising that the superimposition of generally exclusive linguistic, economic, political and temporal layers has also materialised in the spatial organisation of the city and the ways in which it is inhabited. Postwar anthropological studies of 'urban peasants', historical analysis of villages surrounded by cities, and more recently neologisms invented by geographers – 'periurban', 'rurban' and the like – to describe urbanites settling in agricultural contexts have mapped the increasing blur that characterises the traditional rural-urban boundary. In 1968, Yugoslav American anthropologist Andrei Simic conducted fieldwork on rural-urban mobility in Serbia.[6] What comes out of his study is the 'intermediate' dimension of the Yugoslav nation waiting to complete its transformation from a traditional society to a modern industrial state and the 'transitional' nature of Belgrade: 'Physically the city projects an image of striking contrast, with high-rise apartments looming above adobe hovels and collapsing ancient buildings. Traditional and modern dress are evident in city crowds, and animal-drawn vehicles share the streets with automobiles and trucks.'[7] The book discusses rural folkways, and how the urban community is experiencing a process of peasantisation.

Intermediary Society

Fifty years later, Simic's description of Belgrade is still relevant not only to Chisinau, but to an array of cities. The 'intermediary state' stuck between village and city, rural traditions and urban modernity does not seem to be bounded in time. It has become a mode of territorial transformation that cannot be modelled on the mono-directional rural-to-urban evolution characteristic of Western European and North American societies. At times more of a village, and at others more of a city, going back and forth between these two conditions, Chisinau is still today predominantly constituted by urbanites keeping strong ties with the village they come from. The generations of residents that have succeeded one another have kept alive a spatial organisation whose intricacies are such that one constantly passes from metropolitan agitation to pastoral atmosphere, from carefully planted linear boulevards to countryside courtyards, from regular multistorey facades to patched-together shacks and fences. The random growth of trees and bushes; the asphalt eaten away by the grass; the appropriation of public space with furniture, clothes and other objects belonging to the intimate sphere; and the makeshift extensions and fences made of various materials – all these elements contribute to the making of a landscape that breaks the order associated with the design of the city.

This rural mode of living in the heart of the city can be historically explained. Today a city

of over 700,000 people, Chisinau had a peak of 100,000 inhabitants at the turn of last century that fell to 25,000 as a result of the Second World War. The city centre, its extension in the form of a grid planned by the Russian empire in the 19th century, and the neighbouring villages were mostly made of single-storey buildings. In direct relation to the ground, these houses had two facades: urban on the street and rural in the back courtyards. Their position has most recently been identified in 2001 by the Moldovan Institute of Geodesy, Technical Research, and Cadastre (INGEOCAD) on a map where these low-rise houses are marked in yellow to distinguish them from the pink-coloured high-rises. How were these disorganised and semi-derelict structures kept generally intact by fifty years of Soviet planning?

Once again, Moldova's peripheral position explains this: plans drawn in Moscow put their effort into providing a decor for diplomatic delegations and state representatives. As in stage sets, high-rise buildings framed large axes of circulation. On the borders of the Soviet Union where the symbolic translation of power into architecture was at its weakest, what went on behind the scenes did not matter. Additionally, 'from 1958 all construction of

INGEOCAD,
Map of Chisinau,
Moldova,
2001

above: The city comprises the medieval Old Town (1), 19th-century Russian Town (2), Integrated Villages (3), and 1950s high-rise housing blocks (*microrayons*) (4). 68 Sciusev Street is situated between the State University and the National Library (2*) and Odessa Street is adjacent to one of the main parks called the Valley of Roses (3*). The yellow background indicates low-rise buildings, and pink the Soviet high-rise housing. Scale: 1: 10,000.

Makeshift housing,
Odessa Street,
Chisinau,
Moldova,
2012

right: Makeshift housing on a street with no pavements or urban amenities, in a part of the city that was originally a small village community. In the background, the silhouette of the Cosmos Hotel built in the early 1980s reveals the proximity and contrast between the rural patterns and Soviet-era construction.

housing was planned exclusively on virgin land. Furthermore, demolition of existing housing exceeding 2–3 % of the area of new housing was forbidden'.[8] Consequently large-scale housing operations were inserted on the vacant land lying between patches of single-storey rural or semi-rural houses. The latter remained inhabited and untouched independently of their state of maintenance. As a result, and just as with the rest of its temporal, economic and linguistic dimensions, the city is not urban in parts or rural in others. The rural and urban strata are meshed together.

The Persistence of the Vernacular

The rural in Chisinau is neither determined by a form of production and economy (mostly agricultural), nor defined in opposition to urban morphology. As shown on the INGEOCAD map by the pervading yellow colour, single-storey buildings are present in the pattern of Old Town medieval streets, as well as in the blocks drawn by the grid of the Russian city. A walk, map in hand, confirms their existence: residents live close to the ground and rural traits are evident. In this case, these traits epitomise the vernacular, as discussed by John Brinckerhoff Jackson in his book *Discovering the Vernacular Landscape* (1984).[9] Vernacular architecture is 'homemade', it is a relation to the environment, and a way of inhabiting that comes from a knowledge of the land, its climate and topography. Jackson, whose main object of study is American landscape, reflects upon this notion, not only as an attribute of the countryside, but as it can be found in provincial towns and in the suburbia of large cities alike. What defines the vernacular is its opposition to

the political landscape, which is planned and ignorant of the specificity of the land.

Classical urban discourse has focused on Rome, then Berlin and Paris, and later New York and Chicago as epitomes of the city. These principal cities were formed by strong governmental and political mechanisms that led to the recession of the vernacular landscape.[10] Historians have shown that modernisation attempted to unify, regulate and standardise practices and production not only in cities, but also in the countryside.[11] The government in Moldova had only relatively weak economic means to impose an urban order. This combined with the fact that Chisinau residents come from villages, or have families still closely bound to the traditions of the countryside, accounts for the flourishing of this urban rurality. What gives Chisinau a distinct character is the omnipresence of the vernacular at different scales and parts of the city. Its expansion seems to have taken over the city, and explains the saying that 'Chisinau is a capital in the process of becoming a village'.[12]

Today, associations of architects and residents fight for the protection of the Old Town with its characteristic rural attributes, which to them differentiate Chisinau from generic cities. However, the battle is complicated by the fact that the city not only retains the character of a village to be preserved, but is caught in an ongoing process of transformation that assumes a double-fold movement. On the one hand, villagers whose property has acquired real-estate value agree to sell their lots, and invest their money in the high-rise apartments that replace them. On the other, illegal constructions put together by less fortunate rural migrants colonise the vacant land still available within

the metropolitan perimeter. They contribute to the expansion of areas that to some extent are spatially and materially not so different from those identified in the Old Town or the villages encompassed by the city after the war. While the vernacular dimension of some parts of the old Chisinau is accepted by most as characteristic of the city, the response among critics and architects to the ongoing process of ruralisation has been mixed. They tend to distinguish between the long-term inscription of rural settlements in the urban fabric and this more recent manifestation of homemade changes to the urban structure.

Design and Ruralisation

The interest of the intermediary society and its territorial organisation lies in the intimacy that binds the political and vernacular landscapes, and therefore the negotiation that takes place between them. Traditionally, architectural, urban and landscape designs have helped transform the political landscape. But in Chisinau, the space planned by a governmental entity is more or less equal in size to that which has been spontaneously and informally appropriated. How do designers contribute to the understanding and transformation of such an urban context?

The modes of production of these two landscapes are diametrically opposed in the sense that urban design aims to control spatial changes through the discussion and drawing of what should be built, whereas rural appropriation of space comes out unmediated by a process of representation, and as such one may not yet speak of design. This distinction is illustrated in 1980s issues of the architectural magazine *АРХИТЕКТУРА СССР*: models of

Cadastral plan of Chisinau, Moldova, 2016

While the forms of each block are specific to each period – the Russian Town grid on the westernmost side of the detail, the triangles of the Old Town to the northeast, and the contorted streets of the village structure to the southeast – the irregularity and unlikely geometry of the plots and buildings is shared by all. Informal appropriation of space appears in multiple paths, corners and enclaves. Asterisked numbers indicate the places from which the photographs here of Odessa Street and 68 Sciusev Street were taken.

housing towers sit on immaculate slabs on which lawns and paths are painted, while photographs of building sites show tower blocks under construction with country houses in the foreground surrounded by wooden rural fences immersed in spontaneous growth of trees and ivy.

In an article on the relation between 'gestures' and the making of gardens, the French landscape architect Gilles Clément writes that his conviction in plans was never very deep and he often wonders whether he should draw his projects before or after having made them.[13] In a similar fashion, the architect-artist Catherine Rannou has used AutoCAD to represent the evolution of a refuse dump close to an Inuit village in Nunavut, Northern Canada that is built almost entirely of standardised social housing units provided by the Canadian government. Her photographic survey investigates the relation between this standard architecture and the non-standard bricolage invented by a population of originally nomadic hunters.[14]

Both Clément's and Rannou's practices share an interest in situations at the edge of our control (vegetation, the Arctic circle, and the like). They do not cast a vision, or use their landscape and architectural education to draw in order to master them, but rather turn design tools on their head to give a visibility to the fragile balance between the gesture of drawing and the gesture of making; the planned and the spontaneous. This does not only invert the temporal relation between plans and construction, but also opens the activity of designers to a different temporality. Rannou and Clément draw series of plans documenting the transformation of their projects and objects of study over time. They enter a logic of ongoing survey instead of locking shapes on plans, and as such propose an alternative to a trend in rural design whose advocates propose in fact to apply urban design to rural settings.[15]

Catherine Rannou,
Arctic Dump,
Nunavut,
Northern Canada,
2011

One of a series of AutoCAD drawings mapping the evolution of a refuse dump close to Igloolik, an Inuit village in the Arctic. Resources being rare, residents use the place not only to throw away objects, but also to pick up bits and pieces that they recycle for machine repair or house refurnishing. The meticulous survey of its changes maps the vernacular improvements the residents have made to their day-to-day living. The work is part of the online art project 'Igloolik, là où il y a des maisons'.

While optimising land production may be a priority for some strong economic nations, this trend of reorganising rural spaces according to an urban logic of modernisation may be irrelevant to a vast number of 'intermediary societies' that did not even reach the stage of fully fledged industrialisation during the 20th century. Chisinau does not offer a nostalgic trip into bucolic landscapes. Its study helps us to reflect upon the role of architects in an economic and governmental culture that does not have the means to create a strong political landscape. This role may indeed depart from the one-way design-build sequence in which survey always comes before planning, and evolve towards putting in tension the representation of what is to be done (the project) with what is already there (the survey). In this context, drawing and design tools at large may be questioned by architects in order to give a reading of the urban and its transformation by taking into account the intelligence of rural knowledge and its spatial production in our cities. ⌂

Catherine Rannou, Standard and Non Standard, Nunavut, Northern Canada, 2011

The red containers are units provided by the Canadian government to house the newly sedentary population of Inuits at Igloolik. The housing extensions are mostly made of materials found at a nearby refuse dump.

Notes
1. See https://youtu.be/ViCGKctSLm0.
2. For more information on the stakes related to national unification of time, see Peter Galison, *Einstein's Clocks, Poincaré's Maps: Empires of Time*, WW Norton & Company (New York and London), 2003.
3. Deema Kaneff and Monica Heintz, 'Bessarabian Borderlands: One Region, Two States, Multiple Ethnicities', *Anthropology of East Europe Review*, 6, Spring 2006, p 6. Bessarabia is the name of the eastern part of Moldova that after 1991 became the independent Republic of Moldova.
4. *Ibid*, p 7.
5. Violette Rey and Octavian Groza, 'Bulgarie et Roumanie, un "entre-deux" géopolitique dans l'Union Européenne', *L'Espace géographique*, 4, 2008, pp 365–78; Emmanuelle Boulineau, 'Des confins aux voisins. Les relations de l'UE avec les Balkans au prisme des espaces intermédiaires', Géocarrefour, 3, 2014: http://geocarrefour.revues.org/9508.
6. Andrei Simic, *The Peasant Urbanites: A Study of Rural-Urban Mobility in Serbia*, Seminar Press (New York and London), 1973.
7. *Ibid*, p 14.
8. Vladimir Smirnov, *Gradostroitelistvo Moldavii [Moldovan Urbanism]*, trans Kyril Tidmarsh, Cartea moldoveneasca (Chisinau), 1974, p 62.
9. John Brinckerhoff Jackson, *Discovering the Vernacular Landscape*, Yale University Press (New Haven, CT), 1984.
10. Pier Vittorio Aureli, 'City as Political Form: Four Archetypes of Urban Transformation', in Christopher CM Lee and Sam Jacoby (eds), ⌂ *Typological Urbanism: Projective Cities*, January/February (no 1), 2011, pp 32–37.
11. Eugen Weber, *Peasants into Frenchmen: The Modernization of Rural France, 1870–1914*, Stanford University Press (Redwood City, CA), 1976.
12. Pavel Braila, interview with the author, Chisinau, 24 February 2012.
13. Gilles Clément, 'Le geste et le jardin', *Paysage & Aménagement*, 7, June 1986, pp 8–15.
14. For more images from this survey, see www.catherine-rannou.fr/igloolik/en/9/architecture/.
15. Alastair Parvin, 'Open Fields: The New Rural Design Revolution', in Mark Titman (ed), ⌂ *The New Pastoralism: Landscape Into Architecture*, May/June (no 3), 2013, pp 118–25.

Traditionally, architectural, urban and landscape designs have helped transform the political landscape.

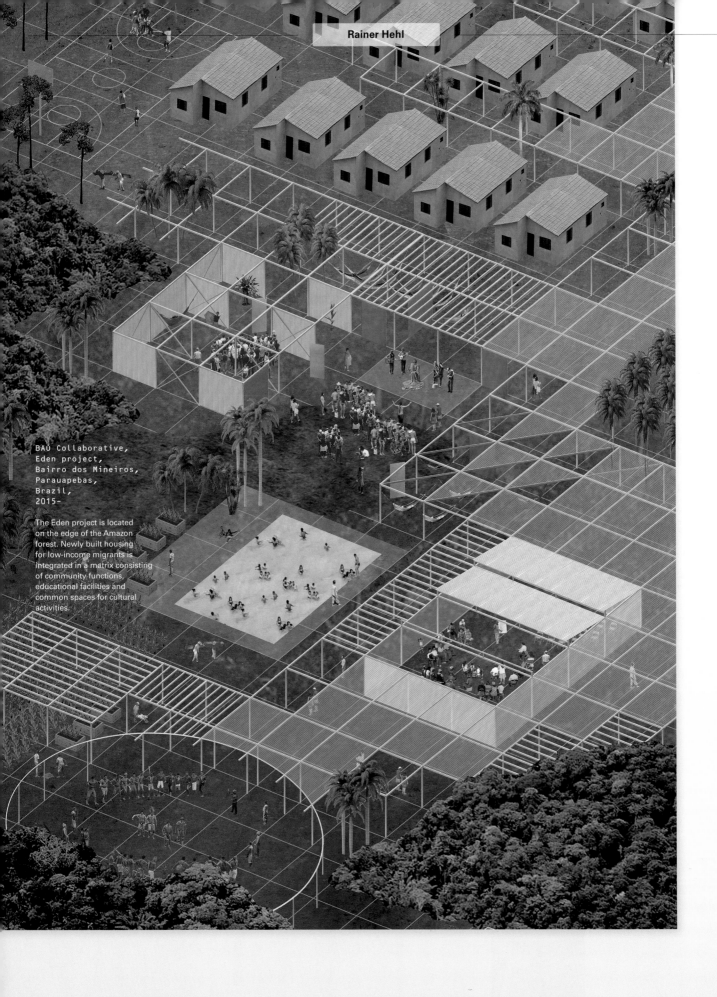

BAU Collaborative,
Eden project,
Bairro dos Mineiros,
Parauapebas,
Brazil,
2015–

The Eden project is located
on the edge of the Amazon
forest. Newly built housing
for low-income migrants is
integrated in a matrix consisting
of community functions,
educational facilities and
common spaces for cultural
activities.

View of Bairro dos Mineiros in Parauapebas looking at the recently finished houses of the mass housing Minha Casa Minha Vida programme, 2013

Established by the federal social housing programme, Bairro dos Mineiros serves as a settlement for workers of the Carajás mine, the biggest open-pit iron-ore mine in the world.

Cultivating the Field in the Global Hinterland

Community Building for Mass Housing in the Amazon Region

The large-scale residential settlements that have sprung up over the last decade to house migrants flocking to join Brazil's burgeoning rural industries are in urgent need of retrofitting with infrastructure and community facilities if they are to become sustainable. To this end, international urban design practice the BAÚ Collaborative has initiated the 'Eden' project – a participatory design process that involves state authorities, local NGOs, residents and social workers. **Rainer Hehl**, a co-founder of BAÚ, outlines the problem, the project, and its test-site: the mining town of Parauapebas.

Of the 19 fastest-growing cities in Brazil where populations have doubled over the past decade, 10 are in the Amazon region. With the proliferation of hydroelectric dams, mechanised soya-bean plantations and intensive mining operations, thousands of migrants have been lured from all over the country in search of jobs and economic stability. Soaring population growth has intensified urbanisation, supported largely by forecasts of robust demand from China and other emerging territories. This has turned the rapidly growing cities in the Amazon into the world's last great settlement frontier. Urbanisation of these rural areas therefore plays a major role in the development of urban centres close to production sites and logistic hubs. While in Brazil most of the attention has focused on how to organise large metropolitan centres, major challenges for future urbanisation can now be found in its rural hinterland. What are the models for these new towns and how can architects and planners play an active role in the design of emerging rural territories?

The 'Eden' project is focused on how community building can be integrated with state-sponsored mass housing. It was initiated by BAÚ Collaborative, an international urban design practice for participatory development in emerging urban territories. Collaborating with local NGOs and state authorities that provide assistance for social organisation, BAÚ is testing new models for the urbanisation of rural areas based on cooperative

Reproduction of mono-functional housing units in Bairro dos Mineiros built of reinforced concrete according to standardised models, 2013

The development of mass housing in Brazil is based on the interests of large-scale construction industries. Mono-functional commuter-settlements are erected in the periphery of the cities where land is cheap.

practice. Through involving residents in the planning process, the project leaders also claim that the design of communities in rural areas relies on: a solid structure of social and technical assistance to support cooperative organisations during planning and the post-occupancy phase; the development of a new type of urbanity that can cope with the dispersed and fragmented nature of rural developments; and an incremental design strategy that acts as a framework for sustainable urban growth.

Based on an exemplary development on a test-site in the Brazilian mining town of Parauapebas, the project is a prototypical case through which to investigate how community building can be fostered through design strategies for upgrading newly built mass-housing settlements by retrofitting them with infrastructure and community facilities.

Frontier Zone of Global Capitalism
There is nothing spectacular about Parauapebas. The torrid expansion of the mining town, located between the impenetrable jungle of the Carajás National Forest and deforested landscape, was not accompanied by the proper development of infrastructure and urban services. Although it has an estimated 250,000 inhabitants, it can barely be recognised as a city. In fact, it's hard to say how many people live in Parauapebas as the numbers are constantly changing. With a growth rate higher than 12 per cent per year and an estimated annual increase

of 30,000 inhabitants, the municipal government finds it difficult to cope with the constant flow of incoming migrants from all over the country. In view of the massive demand for housing, land prices are skyrocketing, leading to aggressive real estate speculation. As a result, prices for former agricultural land transformed into lot divisions are often as high as in metropolitan areas such as Rio de Janeiro or São Paulo.

'In the speculator's dream lay the urban promise – and the urban imperative – of frontier settlement and investment.'[1] What William Cronon described as a theory of economic growth that dominated 19th-century thinking about frontier developments turned, in the case of Parauapebas, into a handicap for any attempt to organise the city according to good urban governance. Buildings here are being built for the market and speculation is impeding the low-income population from finding affordable rents. This also leads to a fragmented and fractured city, where the focus on surplus profits prevents the city from growing in a coordinated and compact manner.

In a place where as many as two homes have to be built each hour to meet surging demand, any intentions to plan the city properly seem futile. In view of this impossible task, the Municipality's solution was to privatise infrastructure. This way, the developer receives the concession to subdivide

BAú Collaborative, workshop, Eden project, Bairro dos Mineiros, Parauapebas, Brazil, 2015–

Self-organised by the community, the workshop is used for repair services and cooperative practice, generating income for the inhabitants of Bairro dos Mineiros.

the land and sell it, if they guarantee the provision of basic infrastructure for water supply, sewage and road access. But what seemed to be a solution for an overburdened Secretariat for Public Works proved to be the real dilemma on the way to a comprehensive planning framework. Meanwhile, the lack of infrastructure and housing provision by public authorities ultimately leads to the proliferation of informal squatter settlements where the lowest segment of the population finds the only affordable alternative.

While favelas in the more central districts of Parauapebas are being gradually removed, they continue to grow along the riverbeds and in proximity to newly built infrastructure. Given the speed of informal development, illegal building activity can be considered an integral component of speculative growth. If both informality and speculation are just different facets of urban production, the frontier town provides a lesson in how urbanisation in the global hinterland can be seen as a by-product of an economy that has other priorities. While mining activity is undertaken with advanced technologies and an impressive mobilisation of labour and logistics, urban development occurs without any of these sophisticated tools. How could these cities benefit from global flows of capital and grow into sustainable settlements rather than being detrimental, yet necessary, by-products of the system?

BAú Collaborative,
workshop, Eden
project,
Bairro dos Mineiros,
Parauapebas,
Brazil,
2015–

Self-organised by the
community, the workshop
is used for repair services
and cooperative practice,
generating income for the
inhabitants of Bairro dos
Mineiros.

Generic Housing Models Versus Specific Adaptations

For local authorities there is not much time to think about the long-term impact of planning given the speed of urban transformation. In order to cope with the massive demand for housing and urban services, the government launched several developments of state-sponsored social housing in Parauapebas, aiming to produce new neighbourhoods for households earning between one and three minimum salaries.[2]

The programme of generic housing production in Brazil was introduced on a massive, national scale with the launch of the social housing scheme Minha Casa Minha Vida (MCMV) in 2009. Tailored to boost the economy after the global financial crisis of 2008, the programme's declared mission was to tackle the housing deficit in the country – an estimated six million units. Within a four-year period, Minha Casa Minha Vida aimed to construct 3.4 million housing units and about half have been built so far. The largest social housing programme in the world, it has been quite successful in giving low-income populations access to housing and, at the same time, attracting foreign investment for its implementation.

Developed by construction companies in remote locations where land is cheap, MCMV settlements stand for everything that goes against good urban planning. The mono-functional commuter settlements are poorly built: they lack public services, collective spaces, greenery, and even commercial units for local supply. As a consequence, the housing units are informally extended immediately after construction, turning into favelas or ghettos. Deficient infrastructure and unstable, bumpy roads have to be upgraded shortly after completion. What was meant to be a solution in many cases turns out to create even more problems. The programme's name, which translates as 'My House My Life', represents the wish to create a new middle class of homeowner-consumers. With the emphasis on privatisation, all aspects concerning the formation of civic centres and public facilities are neglected. Besides the low quality of the MCMV housing models, the goal of the programme simply to provide access to housing for individuals fails to address collective needs and the management of the public realm.

Could the provision of homes for low-income dwellers also provide a basis for building the city – for building an environment that offers civic institutions and public spaces, fostering local identity and a sense of belonging? Like many other state-led social housing programmes, Minha Casa Minha Vida develops standardised and mono-functional settlements that are lacking any kind of

> Due to the fact that fragmentation in rural areas cannot be simply undone, local neighbourhoods have to develop their own service cores that operate independently from the overall logic of the urban system.

urban services. Besides that, facilities for education, healthcare and cultural activities are missing; even the integration of commercial uses within the units is prohibited. The public authorities argue that mixed-use programmes are incompatible with subsidised social housing. As a result, the lively streetscapes that are characteristic of popular neighbourhoods in Brazil are replaced by large-scale, air-conditioned shopping centres. How could these mono-functional commuter-settlements be retrofitted with social and ecological infrastructures that would allow low-income dwellers to establish a communal life? What are the alternatives to a social housing programme that is meant to be the only viable way to cope with the growing masses?

Test Site: Bairro dos Mineiros

As part of the MCMV programme's overall budget, 5 per cent is dedicated to 'entidades' (entities) – social movements and cooperatives – which take care of the planning and construction of their own future neighbourhoods. Instead of serving the interests of the construction market, 'MCMV Entidades' allows the design of neighbourhoods that are developed according to the interests of the future residents. Even though this programme accounts for only a small portion of the total state-sponsored housing production, it provides an opportunity for design developments that are specifically tailored to the needs of the given group or community. The Eden

BAú Collaborative, market, Eden project, Bairro dos Mineiros, Parauapebas, Brazil, 2015-

The covered market serves as a hub for the trading of products from agroforestry and organic farming.

project was established with MCMV Entidades's logic of cooperative development by taking an existing low-income neighbourhood as a test-site.

Bairro dos Mineiros is a new town for 10,000 inhabitants that started construction in 2013 on formerly agricultural land at the periphery of Parauapebas. The houses were built in three phases, with the last phase completed in 2015. Envisioned by the Municipality as an exemplary neighbourhood for low-income workers, it has already turned into a ghetto. Public infrastructure is decaying, community spaces are neglected, crime rates are increasing and public transportation to workplaces is scarce. How can we provide urban services and connect the neighbourhood better to the city? How can we upgrade an area that is newly built? And how can we develop a neighbourhood that acts like a city within the city?

Due to the fact that fragmentation in rural areas cannot be simply undone, local neighbourhoods have to develop their own service cores that operate independently from the overall logic of the urban system. While Parauapebas operates at the periphery of the centres of global capital as an underdeveloped backwater, providing the world with the materials needed to cope with ongoing economic growth, the city in turn creates its own underserviced hinterland. Bairro dos Mineiros can be considered as the

periphery within the periphery: it acts as the final link of a chain that is based on the logic that the level of income serves as a measurement for access to infrastructure. Deprived from sufficient services, the residents of Bairro dos Mineiros are locked in a situation that does not allow economic growth and social mobility. With the goal of retrofitting the settlements with civic functions and an infrastructural grid enabling incremental development of community and commercial uses, the Eden project starts with reassembling the common ground. By redefining infrastructure provision as a tool for social and ecological development, the picture of the neglected rural periphery can be reversed: instead of a dead-end, Bairro dos Mineiros can then be considered as a local centre and as a productive interface between urban and natural environments.

Social, Technical and Design Assistance
What exactly are the protocols and procedures that would guarantee the proliferation of social and ecological sustainability in low-cost housing developments? What are the challenges that we have to face for participatory design developments in rural areas? Even though Brazil has a network of social organisations stemming from a long history of workers' movements and class struggle, these networks do not reach remote areas like Parauapebas. Experience of participatory design previously undertaken in the context of MCMV Entidades has shown that the only reliable anchor for social organisation is represented by churches, charity organisations and a few independent NGOs. In order to hold participatory design meetings with

Aerial view of a typical development in Parauapebas: houses are being built before infrastructure services are installed, 2013

Parauapebas is a mining town situated on the southern edge of the Amazon forest. With more than 12 per cent annual growth the city is ranging among the fastest-growing cities of Brazil.

up to 500 residents, social assistance is needed to mediate between collective needs and individual preoccupations. Given the lack of education and fixation on individual property, participation of low-income populations requires particular attention on teaching how housing production works, how we can conceive the city as a collective project and what differentiates well-designed settlements from generic settlements. As the task of mobilising and instructing the future dwellers about the opportunities of communal living often exceeds the capacities of architects, only close collaboration with social workers enables an inclusive design process. What has been termed in Brazil 'Social Technical Assistance' should be extended as a design practice that involves residents, architects and social workers alike. Participatory design then operates as an open framework that relies on the fact that architectural and urban design is conceived as an integral component of self-organisation.

The Civic Centre as a Field
Once a participatory design process is established, what exactly is the task of the urban designer? Is the role of architecture reduced to the mediation and orchestration of the user's need? While self-organisation plays a crucial part for a development that should be installed and maintained by the residents, the Eden project calls for a design approach that clearly structures urban growth in the future, regardless of individual and collective appropriations. What would be a model that allows for dynamic incremental processes and at the same time directs urban growth in a more sustainable way?

In contrast to neighbourhood development within highly dense urban centres, rural environments have to mediate differently between the private and public spheres. While urbanity in centralised cities is characterised by the polarisation of introversion and public exposure, in rural contexts domestic life is immediately confronted with a dispersed landscape and a scattered network of social relations. What would be the model that provides a sense of civic consciousness while at the same time coping with the fragmented nature of dispersed rural developments? What kind of urbanity can we imagine that does not reproduce the density of urban agglomerations but still provides collective livelihoods with economic means with respect to local resources?

The project for the community centre in Bairro dos Mineiros seeks to overcome the undefined spatial conditions and sparsely established urban infrastructures by establishing a grid that operates as a matrix of public functions. Interspersed between the loosely arranged individual homes and empty plots of neglected landscape, civic infrastructure is conceived as a layer that penetrates the private realm. The generic structure of the framework is programmed according to contextual needs in order to enable places for celebration, for social gathering, for education, for play, for production and for the cultivation of the natural environment. Community building in a place that is neither city nor nature is here conceived as a field of interactions and associations – as an infrastructure that unfolds the potentials of social organisation and as a tool that blurs the boundaries between manmade and natural environments.

View of Parauapebas towards the edge of the Amazon forest, 2013

The rapidly growing mining town is located in close proximity to the biggest open-pit iron-ore mine of the world.

Notes
1. William Cronon refers here to the Boosters' economy of Chicago and the Midwest, which saw the engine of western development in the symbiotic relationship between cities and their surrounding countrysides. William Cronon, *Nature's Metropolis: Chicago and the Great West*, WW Norton (New York), 1992, p 34.
2. Currently the national minimum wage in Brazil is 880 Brazilian reais (equivalent to US$225).

Setting the Frame for Future Urban Growth

In Parauapebas and in many other rural contexts the future remains uncertain. What if mining activity suddenly decreases? Will the city then lose its ground or will it find other alternatives that sustain future growth? While the new towns created by Minha Casa Minha Vida only deliver access to housing, the newly built settlements do not provide any kind of opportunity for income generation. What if the design of rural settlements could also provide a backbone for commercial activities and services developed by the community themselves? Rather than establishing civic centres as punctual interventions throughout the dispersed landscape of the Amazon region, the Eden project is conceived as a matrix that covers the field and assembles the different fragmented parts as a whole. But instead of just being designed as 'hardware' the layer penetrating settlements and nature is conceived as 'software': activities such as local agriculture, education, recreation and cultural programmes guarantee the collective cultivation of the field. The design of the framework is conceived as a process combining an open structure with the practice of 'commoning' by specific user groups and neighbourhood associations. As a prototypical device the structure only becomes active as soon as we anticipate and co-design the performance needed to produce local identities and cultures. And who knows? By designing an open framework we might also lay out the structure that in the future will become a city. ᴆ

Palm

A New Ethics of Visibility for the Production Landscape

The explosion of the palm oil industry in recent decades has transformed vast swathes of the Malaysian and Indonesian countryside. **Milica Topalovic**, Assistant Professor of Architecture and Territorial Planning at ETH Zurich, asserts that the resulting agro-industrial landscapes challenge the very concept of what is rural, and considers how such areas should be conceptualised.

The palm tree is a powerful symbol: a synonym for desirable cities with favourable climates and a waterfront, the key ingredients of urban wealth and leisure landscapes. But it is also a symbol of remote wilderness, of countryside and of agricultural production that has been virtually forgotten. It is now beginning to represent the crucial, if less visible, dynamic reshaping of the rural realm – the growth and globalisation of agro-industrial production that is increasingly consuming land and landscapes around the globe and redefining the traditional meanings of rural or countryside areas.

Moving beyond the traditional notion of the rural is necessary to understand these expanding agro-industrial production landscapes: hinterlands such as palm oil plantations need to be subsumed into our conception of the urban as essential supporting territories that provide vital resources for the cities in which we live.

Architecture and the visual arts also have an important role to play in researching, describing and making visible to the urban dweller the ongoing industrial reorganisation of the rural realm. These territories can no longer be seen as remote, residual or anachronistic: they are crucial areas of global capitalism and of processes of urbanisation. A new ethics of visibility that extends from the urban to the rural is required.

Geography of Paradise
Though the palm family is extensive and diverse, comprising more than 2,500 known species,[1] only a few types fit the ideals of blue sky and sea as tirelessly replicated by American conceptual artist John Baldessari in works such as *Palmtree Seascape* (2010), those Edward Ruscha photographed for *A Few Palm Trees* (1971) or the ones David Hockney painted in his mise-en-scène of *A Bigger Splash* (1967).

As a pictorial motive and a cultural symbol, the palm tree has always occupied Western imagination. In the Book of Genesis it was the Tree of Life, the sacred tree of fertility and longevity, a symbol of spiritual victory over flesh and of peace in the aftermath of conflict. In the Age of Discovery and the colonial era, the palm arrived in the North as a symbol of the exotic and control over remote territories. In the mid-19th century, the popular Palm Houses in Victorian Britain and elsewhere in Europe, such as that designed by Decimus Burton and Richard Turner at Kew Gardens (1844–8), staged miniature palm jungles for European city dwellers in recognition of the ambitions and prestige of prosperous collectors and colonial elites. But soon after, the palm escaped these glass and iron conservatories to conquer coastal holiday resorts anywhere from the English Channel to the Mediterranean, from Torquay to Nice.

The palm has been a modern archetype ever since, one that stands at the intersection of wealth and leisure, marking our increasingly universal desire for tropicality. Urban palm trees grace images of desirable urbanity – residing by poolsides in condominiums and resorts. Synonymous with wealth and power, they are embroidered on both bathrobes and military uniforms. And drawings of palm islands cast an artificial emblem for satellite photography, transforming specific geographies into a common imaginary.

Palms are an ingredient of better cities, a sign of permanent leisure, of early retirement and the Sun Belt – of LAs, Miamis and Dubais everywhere. They give identity to generic cities, which in the words of Rem Koolhaas depend on this 'Edenic residue', whose 'immoral lushness' compensates for their other poverties.[2] Palms are the markers of the contemporary geography of Paradise. But there are other types of palms.

Geography of Production
If classified not according to the principles of botany, but to their place in the geography of urbanisation, then next to the city palm, a wide variety of other types can be distinguished. Among them are the palm species found 'in the wild', the palms of the rural areas, as well as the species of the production forests – the worker palms such as *Elaeis guineensis*, the oil palm.

According to the United Nations (UN) and other sources, the oil palm territory has more than doubled since 1990, and continues to grow at the same pace.[3] Palm oil production currently covers an area the size of England and Wales, most of it located in Malaysia and Indonesia.[4] Major expansion is ongoing in South Asia (Papua New Guinea, Thailand) and in West African countries (Nigeria and the Congo basin), where it will replace rainforest and rural smallholdings, facilitated by local governments and, predictably, the military.[5] Palm oil's exceptional 'cleanliness' – a high yield with very little waste – makes it an ideal generic commodity, together with corn syrup, sugar or soya, a universal ingredient found in a myriad of food products, soaps, detergents and biofuels. Consequently, 90 per cent of its global production is controlled by multinational corporations and traded on financial markets.[6]

The available data adds that the production of a single tree typically averages 30 litres (6.5 gallons) per year, and that per capita annual consumption of palm oil in the European Union is nearly 60 litres (13 gallons). One might imagine the statistically average EU citizen as a patron of two oil palms in Southeast Asia, and the entire EU controlling a palm oil hinterland roughly twice the size of Switzerland.

The issues of individual as well as institutional, public and corporate responsibility for the explosion of palm oil cultivation are frequently invoked.

At the level of corporate responsibility, instruments such as the Roundtable on Sustainable Palm Oil (RSPO) and the 'certified sustainable palm oil' label have been developed since 2004 (almost simultaneously with the EU carbon emissions trading system) to create a common framework of commitment for producers and traders. The criticism of such measures by Greenpeace and other organisations points at the jargon of corporate promises, which though it maintains the appearance of corporate responsibility, in reality has an indefinite execution date. For example, in the most optimistic estimates presented by the producing companies and members of the RSPO, only 20 per cent of actual palm oil production is certified 'sustainable';[7] however, according to stricter social and environmental criteria, a 'sustainable palm oil' substance has never been produced.

At the level of governmental responsibility, the solutions are not readily available either. The sustainability agenda of public institutions is often simplified and narrowed to the 'clean and green' message for cities and their proximate environment, without having the interest or the instruments to reduce the massive, albeit remote ecological consequences of one's consumption patterns.

With corporations and institutions failing to tackle the issue, the responsibility falls to the individual. Critics of capitalism, including Marxist scholar Slavoj Žižek, have pointed out that our culture tends to lay responsibility for the environmental mishaps of the late capitalist economy on the individual citizen-consumer. This, according to Žižek, leads to symbolic but ultimately futile practices of 'ethical consumption'. Individual symbolic acts such as purchasing 'sustainable palm oil' only amount to 'the delusion of green capitalism'.[8]

While the remote consequences of palm oil cultivation are framed in the West in relation to rainforest and biodiversity loss and carbon emissions, the lived realities of the palm oil plantations are nearly invisible and inevitably blurred through press reporting and other available information. Only an occasional disaster might bring them into view: 'Your cooking oil may be contributing to the haze,' reads a billboard in Singapore, hinting at the annual burning of jungle and plantations due for replanting some 200 kilometres (125 miles) eastward on Sumatra. Each year the plantation fires generate a cloud of toxic haze of geopolitical proportions that is capable of covering the region from Singapore to Kuala Lumpur and from Medan to Brunei in hazardous

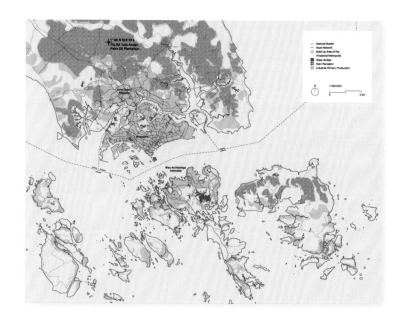

In the most optimistic estimates presented by the producing companies and members of the RSPO, only 20 per cent of actual palm oil production is certified 'sustainable'

Palm oil territories
in the cross-border
metropolitan region of
Singapore,
Johor and the Riau
Archipelago,
2015

above: Singapore is located at the epicentre of the largest palm oil producing region in the world, encompassing the Malay Peninsula, Sumatra and Borneo. Several multinationals involved in palm oil production and trade have their headquarters in Singapore.

Hinterland typologies:
palm oil plantation village
cooperatives,
Taib Andak village cluster,
Johor,
Malaysia,
2015

below: This cluster of palm oil plantation village cooperatives, so-called FELDA schemes, around 50 kilometres (30 miles) northeast of Singapore includes the villages of Sungai Sayong, Bukit Besar, Pasir Raja and Bukit Ramun.

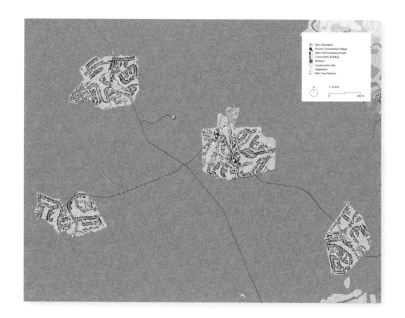

Bas Princen,
Palm oil mill #1,
Taib Andak,
Johor,
Malaysia,
2015

Bas Princen,
Burnt palm oil plantation #9,
Pulai River,
Johor,
Malaysia,
2015

above: The Federal Land Development Authority (FELDA) was established in 1956 with the mission of eradicating poverty by giving land to the landless. Under this programme, over 110,000 'settlers' in Malaysia have become landowners, and shareholders in FELDA.

below: It is believed that the practice of forest burning for the purpose of jungle clearance and renewal of palm oil plantations contributes significantly to global carbon emissions and climate change.

fumes, triggering the international diplomatic blame game, and contributing staggering amounts of carbon emissions to climate change arithmetic. The reliable yearly recurrence of the haze disaster has demonstrated the difficult entanglement of capitalist production, geopolitics and the environment: instead of working towards a solution, governments and the financial sector incentivise palm oil companies and turn a blind eye to practices on the ground. In other words, only through a fundamental restructuring of the entire industry will change be possible.

Investigations of palm oil plantations in Malaysia by the ETH Zurich Architecture of Territory studio have shown that the establishment of the palm oil industry in the country since the mid-1950s (through the so-called Federal Land Development Authority – FELDA – schemes intended to alleviate poverty) has involved massive resettlement programmes that to date have affected more than 110,000 'settlers'.[9] Industrial palm oil cultivation and processing is less labour intensive than any type of traditional fruit cultivation, requiring only about 25 workers per square kilometre. The land has therefore gradually been cleared of its former keepers, usually indigenous populations who have been forced to migrate to cities such as Johor and Kuala Lumpur, catalysing rural-to-urban migration, and directly contributing to the omnipresent patterns of (ostensibly uncontrollable) urban growth in the region. Though initially the local population was replaced with 'settlers' from other parts of the country who worked on the plantations, palm oil production today relies mainly on the more affordable, transnational migrant labour from other Southern and Southeast Asian countries, especially Bangladesh.

Invisible Industrialisation of the Rural
The palm oil hinterlands and other industrial production landscapes that seem to be spreading rapidly and without apparent resistence are still an unfamiliar type of urbanisation that requires closer scrutiny. This is the modern-day *terra incognita* of industrial primary production, hidden from view in areas away from big cities and in clandestine spaces of exception, such as free-trade or export-processing zones, operated under 'special rules' and 'flexible labour' regimes. Seen from a distance, from our self-declared 'post-industrial' and 'post-working-class' societies in the cities of the West (or the North), and mediated through the lenses of popular techno-scientific representations, these production territories seem homogenised and undifferentiated, lacking both social and natural characteristics. They appear as Cartesian, technical landscapes without geographic aberrations, without specificities: a uniform pattern on a map, a grainy texture on Google Earth.

However, it is precisely this ostensibly unspecific geography that is the crucial terrain of the global economy. Tied in to the infrastructures of processing, logistics and trade, its economic utilisation seems to be helped by its abstraction from the concrete realities on the ground. It is easily mystified as a space of 'de-territorialised' and 're-territorialised' production, a part of the technological 'space of flows' and 'weightless economy' of trade. Through such elaborately distorted representations, production spaces are conceptually neutralised from the meanings of locality, place and ground. They become spaces reduced to economic transactions.

The palm oil plantations can no longer be understood as 'rural' in the traditional sense – these territories neither display the continuity of settlement and landownership with the rural areas they came to replace, nor provide any degree of social and economic autonomy (or self-sufficiency) for their residents and workers. They are territories where traditional rural socioeconomic relations have been reorganised in the form of industrial exploitation of the land, whose management and production is positioned within global supply chains. Palm oil territories should be understood as global agro-industrial hinterlands, a concomitant of the global capitalist economy and urbanisation processes. The rural is becoming completely industrialised and urbanised.

Representing and Designing Production Landscapes

Ultimately, how should we perceive and conceptualise the territories of the palm oil production forests? More broadly, how can we understand the spaces of the world's agro-industrial hinterlands? What are the possibilities in these landscapes for critical (policy) interventions and for design? How might design become a tool for rethinking issues raised by palm oil production?

A precondition for any design – and for change through design – is the cultural visibility and clear conceptualisation of a given issue. However, the case here is not only that palm oil landscapes are remote and unknown to the West, but that (industrial) labour and production in the West itself are also generally removed and hidden from view. In fact, the 'disappearance of labour and production from the broader social imaginary' constitutes a widespread cultural symptom of the 'post-industrial' world.[10]

Despite the diverse traditions of depicting labour and production in modern art – ranging from photography documenting the transformation of the American frontier during the second half of the 19th century, to social-realist art centred on the worker as the New

Soviet man in the 1920s and 1930s, and the conceptual and minimal works of Bernd and Hilla Becher that record the disappearance of industrial architecture in the 1960s and 1970s – the later 20th century marked a shift in cultural production. Mirroring the traumatic deindustrialisation of the West that had begun in the 1960s, production and labour as categories of artistic engagement progressively diminished. Especially during the 1980s and early 1990s, in the post-industrial society and within Postmodernist preoccupations with popular culture, commodity aesthetics, identity, gender and so on, 'large segments of labour and production were in fact concealed from common view since they were exported to the geo-political "margins"'.[11]

Only in the late 1990s did a renewed interest in the economic subject, this time globalised commodity production and distribution, sporadically begin to return to North American and Western European art. Photographic works as distinct from each other as Allan Sekula's text-image essays on the global shipping industry (*Fish Story*, 1995) and later Andreas Gursky's monumental scenes of manufacturing (*Nha Trang*, Vietnam, 2004) share the same objective of seeking an image for the ostensibly endless, volatile and un-mappable subject of global capitalism. It could be argued that such efforts continue today and are critical, as production landscapes in particular remain abstract, distant and hidden from view. The scale, specificities and lived realities of territories such as the palm oil production forests are still largely incomprehensible or unknown. How, then, could an ethics of visibility be extended from cities to these territories? How can one create an 'index of the hidden and the unfamiliar' for the production forests?[12]

There is no doubt that production landscapes are no longer the 'absolute spaces' of nature they once were. They are socially produced spaces, a 'second nature' shaped by human activity, conceptualised and inscribed into contemporary forms of representation. This may seem to render any exploration dubious, and curiosity itself superfluous. In 1973, the Italian artist and photographer Luigi Ghirri pointed to this lack of curiosity for exploring the second nature when he wrote: 'By now, all the paradise islands dear to literature and to our hopes have already been described, and the only possible discovery or journey seems to be that of discovering the discovery already made.'[13] However, he also suggested that this perception is incomplete, and actually the opposite is true: 'Even within the most codified world' of the 'already-lived and seemingly totalising experience', 'infinite readings … are always possible'.[14] The production landscapes should therefore be seen as a new

Bas Princen, *Oil palm production forest #7 and #6, Taib Andak, Johor, Malaysia,* 2013

An image of the oil palm should not be mistaken for the icon of tropicality and leisure, but it should also not be dismissed as a symbol of indifference and hypertrophy of global consumption. Instead, it should be seen as a marker of under-represented and unfamiliar hinterland geographies that need to be remapped.

Text © 2016 John Wiley & Sons Ltd. Images: p 42 © Estate of Luigi Ghirri, courtesy Matthew Marks Gallery; p 44 © Assistant Professorship of Architecture and Territorial Planning ETH Zurich DARCH. Map development: Karoline Kostka, plan: Ani Vihervaara; p 45–7 © Bas Princen

frontier for launching the second Age of Discovery,[15] provoking a new kind of urge to explore the landscapes of our planet.

Furthermore, there is a need 'to resist a perception … that neither the self nor the group has any real power to effect change (of global capitalism), that someone else far away is always preventing it … in the larger network of seemingly inhuman, cybernetic global social relations'.[16] Global capitalism is not a Cartesian space nor the infinity of Spinoza. And though it sometimes feels that way, this can only be grounds for greater curiosity rather than inertia.

The process of industrial and urban reorganisation of former rural and natural areas, as in the case of palm oil production, has completely transformed the meaning that notions of the rural and the countryside used to hold. The rural has disappeared: it has become a conceptual black box and an unfamiliar geography, quietly transformed through less familiar, centripetal forces of urbanisation working away from the large centres. The characteristics of these territories – social, cultural, morphological and typological – are yet to be discovered, described and named. The new concepts and representations that will substitute the exhausted notion of the rural will have to show that industrial landscapes such as palm oil plantations are essential parts of our cities – they are the city. This will require thinking, imagining, designing and governing at a larger, transnational and planetary scale, which will be reflected in the locality. ∆

Notes
1. 'Virtual Palm Encyclopaedia': www.plantapalm.com/vpe/introduction/vpe_introduction.htm.
2. Rem Koolhaas, 'Generic City', *S,M,L,XL*, 010 Publishers (Rotterdam), 1995, pp 1248–68.
3. United Nations Environment Programme (UNEP) Global Environmental Alert Service (GEAS), 'Oil Palm Plantations: Threats and Opportunities for Tropical Ecosystems', December 2011: www.unep.org/geas; World Rainforest Movement, *Oil Palm: From Cosmetics to Biodiesel – Colonization Lives On*, 2006: wrm.org.uy/books-and-briefings/oil-palm-from-cosmetics-to-biodiesel-colonization-lives-on/
4. Food and Agriculture Organization of the United Nations (FAOSTAT) online statistical service, data for 2013: http://faostat.fao.org/site/567/default.aspx#ancor.
5. World Rainforest Movement, *op cit*.
6. UNEP, *op cit*.
7. Roundtable on Sustainable Palm Oil (RSPO): www.rspo.org/about.
8. Slavoj Žižek, 'The Delusion of Green Capitalism', lecture, The Graduate Center, City University of New York (CUNY), 4 April 2011: www.youtube.com/watch?v=yzcfsq1_bt8.
9. Milica Topalovic, Martin Knüsel and Marcel Jäggi (eds), *Architecture of Territory: Hinterland – Singapore, Johor, Riau Archipelago*, studio report, ETH Zurich (Singapore), 2013, pp 64–77.
10. Bill Roberts, 'Production in View: Allan Sekula's *Fish Story* and the Thawing of Postmodernism', *Tate Papers*, 18, Autumn 2012: www.tate.org.uk/research/publications/tate-papers/production-view-allan-sekulas-fish-story-and-thawing-postmodernism
11. *Ibid*.
12. Taryn Simon *et al*, *Taryn Simon: An American Index of the Hidden and the Unfamiliar*, Hatje Cantz (Stuttgart), 2008.
13. Luigi Ghirri, *Atlante*, Charta (Milan), 2000, back cover (book based on Ghirri's *Atlante* photographic artwork produced in 1973).
14. *Ibid*.
15. Martha Karen, 'The Master Interviewer: Introduction', interview with Hans Ulrich Obrist, *Surface Magazine*, 104, 2013, pp 124–33.
16. Fredric Jameson and Masao Miyoshi (eds), *The Cultures of Globalization*, Duke University Press (Durham, NC and London), 1998, p 352.

David Grahame Shane

Notes on Villages as a Global Condition

It may seem that rural villages – the basic units of settlement for millennia since humankind first began to tend the land – have been thoroughly usurped by the massive rise in urbanisation over the last centuries. But is this really the case? Tracing the emergence of urbanism and its perception from Aristotle to today, lecturer and writer **David Grahame Shane** reveals the role that the village model continues to play in both the developing and the developed world – including within the much-discussed phenomenon of megacities.

What can the future of the agricultural village be in the 21st century? After forming the basic human settlement for some 8,000 years since the agricultural revolution took place in the Neolithic period, the village has receded at an incredibly rapid pace over the last half century. Only 70 years ago the majority of the global population was still employed in agriculture, even in countries like Italy, France, Germany, Sweden, Denmark, Portugal and Spain, the nation states at the heart of the European empires.[1] The USSR and China also held enormous populations of ex-serfs and peasants who were tied to the land in the Soviet system and later the Chinese *hukou* system that limited people's movement from villages to cities. In colonial Latin America, plantations and villages held the majority of the continent's population in 1945. Today in India, two-thirds of the population still resides in country villages (a complex political category), often illiterate and without modern sanitation or electricity, like in Sub-Saharan Africa.

Villages and the Agricultural Revolution

Humanity's shift from hunter-gatherers to agricultural cultivators involved clustering groups as labourers in village systems to develop the potential of the territory. Traditional village vernacular forms vary across the globe, but are related in their spacing to the carrying capacity of the land. Paul Oliver has described how the landscape capacity, materials, topography, climate and materials all contributed to the vernacular styles of subsistence farming and village formation.[2] In Britain, as elsewhere in Europe, there was a long tradition of village analysis defining a very functional and working non-picturesque vision of urban villages as the basis of human culture from ancient times of subsistence farming, to the medieval feudal system, and then Enlightenment reforms in larger estates and eventually mechanisation in the 19th century.[3] The story continues in the 20th century into the post-colonial cult of villages as the basis of building new peasant-based nations, in Mao's China, Gandhi's India, Nkrumah's Ghana or Sukarno's Indonesia. The 'Green Revolution' of biotech seeds and petrochemical fertilisers continues this village evolutionary narrative into the present.

Industrial village:
New Lanark,
Lanarkshire,
Scotland,
2006

below left: New Lanark became one of the most productive, hydro-powered cotton-mill complexes in Britain in the 1790s, operating day and night under the management of Robert Owen, the pioneering Socialist owner who lived on site and created model housing with a shop, school and infirmary for his 2,000 workers. Production ceased in 1968, and after a period of decay the New Lanark Trust developed the complex as a UNESCO World Heritage site.

Agricultural village:
Hawkshead,
Cumbria,
England,
2014

below right: An important sheep and wool market village in the Middle Ages, Hawkshead was later the birthplace of the Romantic poet William Wordsworth, as well as home to William Heelis, the husband of children's author and illustrator Beatrix Potter. The Potters were early supporters of the British National Trust and sought to conserve the village and its agricultural surroundings in the 1910s.

Agricultural villages that once stood outside the city and its walls could become engulfed by urban expansion. Indeed, Aristotle described a city as an aggregation of villages.[4] These engulfed villages housed many not welcome in the modern city, and modern planners considered them slums because of their poverty and insanitary crowding, often associated with agricultural streambeds, field divisions and once-remote hilltop situations. People often moved between the old agricultural village and the industrial city, a migration that might include (as in India and China today) mass migrations back to home villages at harvest or festival time.

Villages, Industry and the Metropolis in the Modern Nation State

The wealth of the villages in the countryside, their excess labour and production, provided the basis for the emergence of cities and the capital formation of their merchants and landowners. In *Cities in Evolution* (1915), the biologist Patrick Geddes drew a 'Valley Section' diagram stretching from mountain source to delta estuary, describing the geography of villages, towns and cities in relation to the occupants' trades, resources and skills, seeing the whole topographical territory as a regional entity.[5] Here, a hierarchy of towns extracted wealth from villages and sent it from the hinterland to the great port city, the delta city at the river mouth, meeting the sea and oceanic trade, creating the metropolis, heart of the empire.

Early in the Industrial Revolution, cottage industries and village industrial production provided work for agricultural families outside harvest time, setting in motion the evolution of the factory system of concentrated labour in industrial villages like New Lanark outside Glasgow in Scotland.[6] In the 1790s, the early industrial reformer Robert Owen established a system of multistorey factory mill buildings here that ran day and night, powered by hydropower from a nearby waterfall. To house the workers, he designed small apartment buildings along a village street and square, with a school also providing daycare for children, a doctor's surgery and an infirmary, a meeting house and company store. Workers of both genders could take evening classes in the school building, and New Lanark provided Britain with many leaders in the cooperative and labour movements. In the 1820s Owen moved to New Harmony in Illinois in a failed attempt to replicate his success in Lanarkshire, which had made him a millionaire, in America.

Analysis of villages in megablock system in Le Corbusier's 1952 Chandigarh New Town Plan, Northern India, 2011

In Le Corbusier's 1952 plan for Chandigarh in northern India, five pre-existing villages were shown. In later revisions the villages disrupted the normal 1.6 x 2.4 kilometre (1 x 1.5 mile) neighbourhood megablock system (shown enlarged in the upper half of the drawing here) intended to contain four village neighbourhood units (shown in grey) around a central park (shown in green), a school and small commercial centre. In the lower half of the illustration, the small state campus stood isolated to the north of the megablock grid system, while the commercial market area (shown in red) occupied the centre, with linear parks running north to south (shown in green) along streambeds. Redrawn from the original by David Grahame Shane and Uri Wegman.

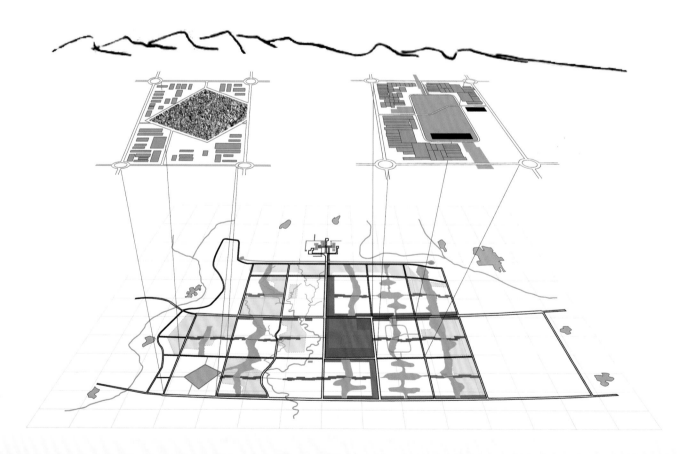

Other entrepreneurs, reformers and European nation states also followed this modern village approach to industrialisation, often in the hope of controlling the workers. In the Soviet system, for instance, the profit from the sale of agricultural produce of the newly collectivised Soviet village brigades provided the capital for the rapid industrialisation of the USSR in the 1930s in the Soviet industrial new towns under Stalin, while Henry Ford provided the blueprints for some of the giant factories. In 1933, Walter Christaller mapped the ideal theory of networks of villages around a town as part of his Central Place theory, later transformed into networks of villages proposed for Nazi Germany as a defence against the USSR in land taken from Poland, part of the German city-landscape, or *Stadtlandschaft*, tradition.[7] Chairman Mao later followed the same state planning model with Chinese characteristics after his nationalisation of the land and collectivisation of villages to build rural *danwei* – industrial villages and small industrial towns housing industrial workers' brigades drawn from the excess peasant labour force.[8]

Networks of Villages in the Megalopolis and the Fragmented Metropolis

Colonial planners and Modernist designers of new towns often ignored old networks of villages and their environmental register. Le Corbusier, for instance, did not show the network of five pre-existing villages on the site of Chandigarh, India, with the result that his 1952 plan had to be adapted by his cousin Pierre Jeanneret, with Fry and Drew of London, to accommodate the villages in the 1950s. Modern state planners preferred or imagined a tabula rasa with no village settlements. Planners demolished the fishing village of Tsuen Wan that gave its name to the first Hong Kong new town in the 1960s in stages, as inhabitants and immigrants living on boats in the bay were displaced to new blocks of merchants' shophouse streets with residences above stores on nearby landfill, and then moved to large modern housing estates. Sha Tin and later Hong Kong new towns preserved the villages as historic conservation areas inside the Los Angeles-style megablocks of the new auto-based city, as did Milton Keynes, the last British new town of the early 1970s.

The switch from rail- to highway, described by Jean Gottmann in *Megalopolis* (1961), further developed the concept of the city territory of the Geddes 'Valley Section' to include the

Analysis of villages in megablock system in Llewellyn-Davies, Weeks, Forestier-Walker and Bor's 1967-8 Milton Keynes New Town Plan, Buckinghamshire, England, 2011

In the 1967– 8 New Town Plan for Milton Keynes, UK, the 14 pre-existing villages were subject to historic preservation orders limiting their growth (shown in brown), often linked to streambed parkland greenbelts (shown in green). The kilometre-square planned road matrix grid created hybrid megablocks that might contain a village, a park and an industrial estate as well as low-density single-family housing estates. A large shopping mall forms the civic centre. Redrawn from the original by David Grahame Shane and Uri Wegman.

Kampung areas
Non-kampung (public buildings, malls, office blocks)
Non-kampung (low-rise commercial, mixed use)
Non-kampung (residential, mixed use)

Stephen Cairns and
Eva Friedrich,
Kampung City,
Jakarta,
Indonesia,
2015

Professor Stephen Cairns and
Eva Friedrich mapped the origins
of the Jakarta *desakota* (village
city) system in the original Dutch
Kampung village settlements,
encouraged for spice growing
and as labour pools close beside
the Dutch East India Company's
original colonial settlement of
Battavia. Their research showed
that much of the original
agricultural land shown on 1930s
maps (shown in green) and the
villages (shown in grey) still
remains today in the midst of the
booming, post-colonial megacity
fragments (with large intrusions
shown in red).

whole Northeastern Seaboard of the US containing 34 million people, incorporating many agricultural areas, networks of villages, forests and small towns.[9] Against this jump in scale and expanded field, the journalist Jane Jacobs defended the urban West Village as a small-scale historic, local enclave, writing in praise of the street life of the diverse community.[10] This defence of the urban village in the auto age resonated widely in the Anglo-Saxon world. Kevin Lynch, for instance, sought to invent a new visual language to analyse the historical city as a series of village-like local neighbourhood 'districts', enclaves or fragments, leading to Colin Rowe and Fred Koetter's 'Collage City' (1975).[11]

In Asia, the geographer Terry McGee began a similar questioning of the Modernist tabula-rasa megablock, highlighting the ancient 'village city' (*desakota*) tradition of migration and exchange between city and countryside in Indonesia.[12] There the Dutch colonialists had accepted and mixed agriculture, canals and the colonial city in the fertile rice paddies, fish farms and orchards surrounding Jakarta (a hybrid continuing to this day).[13] In the 1990s and 2000s McGee and his associates tracked how the increasing globalisation and outsourcing of labour placed big-box factories, warehouses and stores, and even gated communities in this fertile agricultural urban mix to soak up local and global immigrant labour and capital around the edges of the major Southeast Asian delta cities.

Multiple Village Networks in the Contemporary Megacity and Metacity

Over time, McGee described the emergence of a new form of city as an expanded field of multiple villages widely distributed across a peri-urban territory. The village networks form a constellation like a complex enclave system, an expanded version of my fragmentary metropolis category, as theorised in a compact form by Rowe and Koetter in 'Collage City'. Oswald Mathias Ungers and Rem Koolhaas imagined this system as widely distributed islands of urbanity in shrinking, landscaped Berlin in their Archipelago City project (also in the 1970s).[14] Janice Perlman coined the term 'megacity' to describe the Latin American growth pattern of Rio, where migrants from the countryside had self-built 60 per cent of the city of 8 million in favelas – illegal village-like clusters, often originally with space for agriculture.[15] Like McGee, Perlman tracked the lives of the inhabitants over time and the growth of this pattern worldwide. She founded the 'Mega-Cities Project' in 1988, convincing the United Nations to accept the category. The UN now recognises megacities as those with up to 100 million inhabitants.

Terry McGee,
Spatial configuration
of Southeast Asian
mega-urban region,
c 2000

Professor Terry McGee described the 150-kilometre (93-mile) wide band around the periphery of Southeast Asia's port cities – often located in major rice-producing delta areas like Shanghai or Jakarta – as *desakota* (Indonesian for 'village city'). Here, excess labour and capital formation is flexible, and either able to work the land, enter factories when the global system requires or even work in call centres or back-office banking if the literacy level is high enough. This flexibility results in strange juxtapositions and hybrid situations in the extended rururban territory.

The emergence of a new form of city as an expanded field of multiple villages widely distributed across a peri-urban territory.

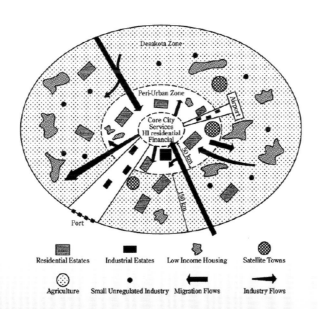

While the extended village favelas of the Latin American megacities might lack basic services, sanitation and water supplies, their inhabitants did find electrical supplies, satellite dishes, televisions and later cellphones and smartphones. They were part of the 'metacity', users and creators of mass media and personal information systems. In 2000, the Dutch group MVRDV coined the term 'metacity' to describe all the information about human life on earth that they projected into a giant data cube, Datatown, so that the land area of the cities represented formed one layer, agriculture another area, forest another area, the sea another layer and so on.[16] This massive data cube symbolised an information revolution that endowed individuals with the power to choose and to interact with each other, much different from the 'global village' of media consumers forecast by Marshall McLuhan (1962) or the big-data processing proposed in the corporate 'smart city'.[17]

The villages of Hong Kong and Shenzhen, and others found in close proximity to the modern new towns of China or India, represent an unintended consequence of the metacity and megacity in Asia. MVRDV hypothesised a new form of 'vertical village',[18] created by informed consumers rather than top-down by state agencies. The model is based on the network of unregulated urban villages of China, with their mini skyscrapers, trapped inside new towns such as Shenzhen (first described by Urbanus in 2006).[19] There is now an expanding literature on 'villages in the city', with authors emphasising the self-organising and flexible bottom-up initiatives of the villagers in the face of fast growth.[20] Agricultural villages have again

Analysis of villages in megablock system in Llewellyn-Davies, Weeks, Forestier-Walker and Bor's 1990 Shenzhen New Town Plan, Guangdong Province, China, 2011

The Shenzhen New Town Plan included 20 villages in its centre that were not subject to planning controls. The 800 x 800 metre (2,625 x 2,625 foot) megablock road grid could contain new high-rise residential and office estates beside factories and the Mao village communes captured by the city (shown in brown). In the north is a mountain park (shown in green) with a statue of Chairman Deng (the initiator of market reform in China) facing down an axis (shown in red) to the open city hall, central park (shown in grey), stock exchange and trade exhibition centre. Redrawn from the original by David Grahame Shane and Uri Wegman.

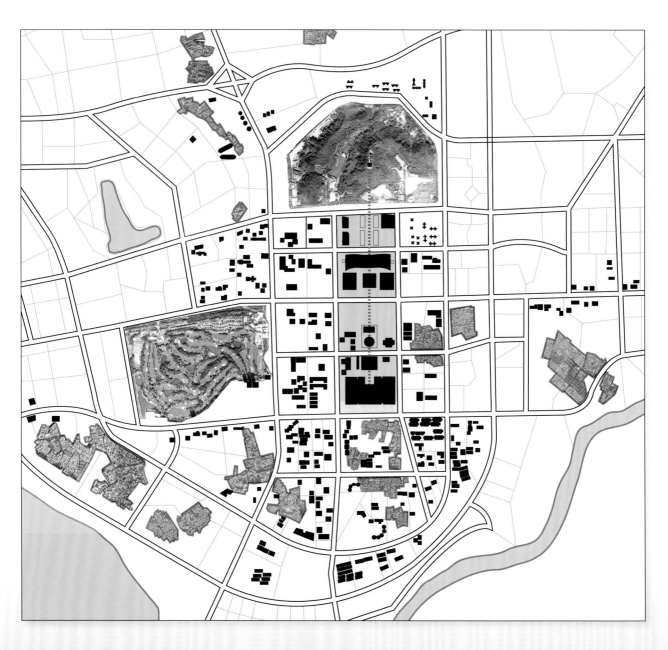

emerged as the foundation of an intense and high-density urbanism, playing a role in capital formation linked now both by ancient family and personal ties, and by the modern mobility and communication systems of the metacity/megacity.

This Southeast Asian *desakota* village city pattern of networked villages also appears as a widely dispersed garden-city form of low-density urbanism, sometimes described as 'landscape urbanism' in the US or in a more dystopian European ecological scenario of 'transition towns' allied with a 'Territorialist School' advocating networks of ecovillages. These European ecovillages appear as neo-medieval utopias riding an 'energy descent' back into local food production based on permaculture and artisanal industry. American versions by Pliny Fisk are more hi-tech, dealing with resource depletion and the impact of climate change, and include an Emergency Village Pac (a flat-pack village housing and services system that could easily be delivered to crisis areas) for the UN.[21]

More recently, in 2013 Paola Vigano advocated the even distribution of highly differentiated, small-town or village-like urban clusters forming a more hopeful and resilient 'Horizontal Metropolis' across an extended field shaped by topography and infrastructure. This urban territory included as exceptions previous village settlements, agriculture and one giant infrastructural service node for every 4 million of the population. Vigano emphasised the lack of hierarchy and global reach of the concept in an École polytechnique fédérale de Lausanne (EPFL) conference in 2015, linking back to Geddes, Gottmann and McGee.[22]

Urbanus,
Heyuan Block,
Gangxia Village,
Shenzhen,
China,
2005

The pre-existing Mao-era agricultural collectives were exempt from the planning regulations of the Shenzhen New Town in the first Special Economic Zone (SEZ) besides Hong Kong. As a result they grew into mini-skyscraper villages to house 60 per cent of the unofficial immigrant workers. Urbanus's study of the Shenzhen urban villages proposes improving living conditions through rooftop additions: blue for water storage and fish ponds; green for gardens, orchards and parks; yellow and orange for communal facilities, schools, bath houses, libraries and galleries; and red for elevator cores.

Designing for Villages in an Extended Urban Field

In the extended field of the megacity/metacity, villages form the basis for multiple hybrid forms of fragmented urbanism in a vast new urban constellation. Villages contain and reflect a shifting dynamic of personal and corporate choices forming small settlement clusters, micro-sized, mixed-use, hybrid live-work versions of the fragmented metropolis enclave system of the 1970s, but now stretched over a *desakota*-scale city territory thanks to personal and corporate communication and transportation systems.

The problem for designers is how to work with the informed multitude of inhabitants of vast village territories and their choices. The self-governing dynamic of the village community is crucial, even if it also involves a virtual dimension that may span the world. The second problem for designers is how to interface with the megastructures of the Modernist state-designed top-down city, the giant infrastructures, the megablocks and big-box elements that land in the *desakota* city-territory with their own logistical dynamic.

It is clear that the traditional role of villages as the basis for a wider urban life has survived in a new recombinant, informational and material form. The post-2008 Great Recession and global market crisis mean that global rururban villages remain an important resource and places of critical resistance in an emerging new urban system. ◮

MVRDV,
Vertical Village,
Taipei,
Taiwan,
2012

Ever since the demolition of the Hong Kong 'City of Darkness' in Kowloon in 1994, MVRDV's Winy Maas has pursued the idea of hyper-dense, hybrid programming in Vertical Villages. In this studio exercise in Taiwan, each hybrid function is colour coded and given a specific shape, then thrown together in a vertical combination. Students produced many variations, experimenting with recombinant codes, all removed from any topographic or urban context.

Notes

1. Tony Judt, *Post war: A History of Europe Since 1945*, Penguin (London), 2006, p 327.
2. Paul Oliver, *Dwellings: The Vernacular House Worldwide*, Phaidon (London), 1987.
3. Thomas Sharp, *The Anatomy of the Village*, Penguin (London), 1946 or William George Hoskins, *The Making of the English Landscape*, Hodder & Stoughton (London), 1955.
4. Spiro Kostof, *The City Shaped: Urban Patterns and Meanings Through History*, Bullfinch (New York), 1991, pp 38–9.
5. Patrick Geddes, *Cities in Evolution*, Williams and Norgate (London), 1915.
6. Ian Donnachie and George Hewitt, *Historic New Lanark: The Dale and Owen Industrial Community Since 1785*, Edinburgh University Press (Edinburgh), 1993.
7. Mechtild Rössler, 'Applied Geography and Area Research in Nazi Society: Central Place Theory and Planning, 1935–1945', *Environment and Planning D: Society and Space 7*, 1989, pp 419–31.
8. David Bray, *Social Space and Governance in Urban China: The Danwei System from Origins to Reform*, Stanford University Press (Stanford, CA), 2005.
9. Jean Gottmann, *Megalopolis*, 20th Century Fund (New York), 1961.
10. Jane Jacobs, *The Death and Life of Great American Cities*, Vintage (New York), 1961.
11. Gordon Cullen, *The Concise Townscape*, Architectural Press (London), 1962; Kevin Lynch, *The Image of the City*, MIT Press (Cambridge, MA), 1962; Colin Rowe and Fred Koetter, 'Collage City', *Architectural Review*, 942, 1975, pp 66–91.
12. Terry McGee, *The Urbanization Process in the Third World*, Bell and Sons (London), 1971; Terry McGee, 'The Emergence of Desakota Regions in Asia: Expanding a Hypothesis', in Norton Sydney Ginsburg, Bruce Koppel and TG McGee (eds), *The Extended Metropolis: Settlement Transition in Asia*, University of Hawaii Press (Honolulu, HI), 1991, pp 3– 25; Terry McGee, George CS Lin, Andrew M Marton, Mark YL Wang and Jiaping Wu, *China's Urban Space: Development Under Market Socialism*, Routledge (London), 2007; Terry McGee, *The Spatiality of Urbanization: The Policy Challenges of Mega-Urban and Desakota Regions of Southeast Asia*, UNU-IAS Working Paper (161), United Nations University Institute of Advanced Studies (Tokyo), 2009.
13. Stephen Cairns and Eva Friedrich, 'Kampung City', in Stephen Cairns and Dirk Hebel (eds), *Future Cities Laboratory Magazine*, 2, ETH/FCL (Singapore), 2014, pp 44–53.
14. Oswald Mathias Ungers and Rem Koolhaas, *The City in the City – Berlin: A Green Archipelago*, eds Florian Hertweck and Sébastien Marot, Lars Müller (Zurich), 1977.
15. Janice Perlman, *The Myth of Marginality; Urban Poverty and Politics in Rio de Janeiro*, University of California Press (Berkeley, CA), 1976, and Janice Perlman, *Favela: Four Decades of Living on the Edge in Rio*, Oxford University Press (Oxford), 2010.
16. MVRDV, *Metacity/Datatown*, NAi (Rotterdam), 2000.
17. Marshall McLuhan, *The Gutenberg Galaxy*, University of Toronto Press (Toronto), 1962, p 31, and Yochi Benkler, 'The Wealth of Networks: How Social Production Transforms Markets and Freedom', 2006: www.jus.uio.no/sisu/the_wealth_of_networks.yochai_benkler/portrait.a4.pdf.
18. MVRDV, Vertical Village (2008): www.vertical-village.com/about/
19. Urbanus, *Village/City, City/Village*, Urbanus (Shenzhen), 2006.
20. Kelly Shannon, Bruno De Meulder and Yanliu Lin (eds), *Village in the City: Asian Variations of Urbanisms of Inclusion*, University of Chicago Press (Chicago, IL), 2014; Margaret Crawford and Jun Wu, 'The Beginning of the End: Planning the Destruction of Guangzhou's Urban Villages', in Stefan Al (ed), *Villages in the City: A Guide to South China's Informal Settlements*, HKU Press (Hong Kong), 2014, pp 19–28; and Juan Du, 'Shenzhen: Urban Myth of a New Contemporary Chinese City', *Journal of Architectural Education*, 63, 2, 2009, pp 65–6.
21. Charles Waldheim (ed), *The Landscape Urbanism Reader*, Princeton Architectural Press (New York), 2005, and Philippe Vandenbroeck and Michiel Dehaene, 'Cityscapes for the Post-Carbon Age: The Small City as Localised Utopia', *Oase 89*, February 2013, pp 80–93. For Pliny Fisk, see Paul Downton, *Ecopolis: Architecture and Cities for a Changing Climate*, Springer (Dordrecht), 2008, pp 114–16, and Center For Maximum Potential Building Systems: www.cmpbs.org/cmpbs.html.
22. Paola Vigano, 'The Horizontal Metropolis and Gloeden's Diagrams: Two Parallel Stories', *Oase 89*, February 2013, pp 94–111. See also the EPFL 'Horizontal Metropolis' symposium, 2015: http://horizontalmetropolis.epfl.ch, as well as https://portal.klewel.com/watch/webcast/the-horizontal-metropolis/ and http://128.178.64.26/lab-u/wp-content/uploads/2015/02/HM_Proceedings_final_light.pdf.

Paola Vigano, 'Horizontal Metropolis' conference poster, École polytechnique fédérale de Lausanne (EPFL), Lausanne, Switzerland, 2015

This map emphasises the global reach of the 'Horizontal Metropolis' concept, including the American megalopolis, Asian *desakota* and Latin American megacities, as well as European city territory regions. The conference speakers, PhD participants and exhibition added great depth to this debate. Vigano sees the Horizontal Metropolis as a field of small, varied settlement clusters, including past villages and agricultural belts, widely distributed over a city territory, with modern communication and transportation infrastructures.

In the extended field of the megacity/metacity, villages form the basis for multiple hybrid forms of fragmented urbanism in a vast new urban constellation.

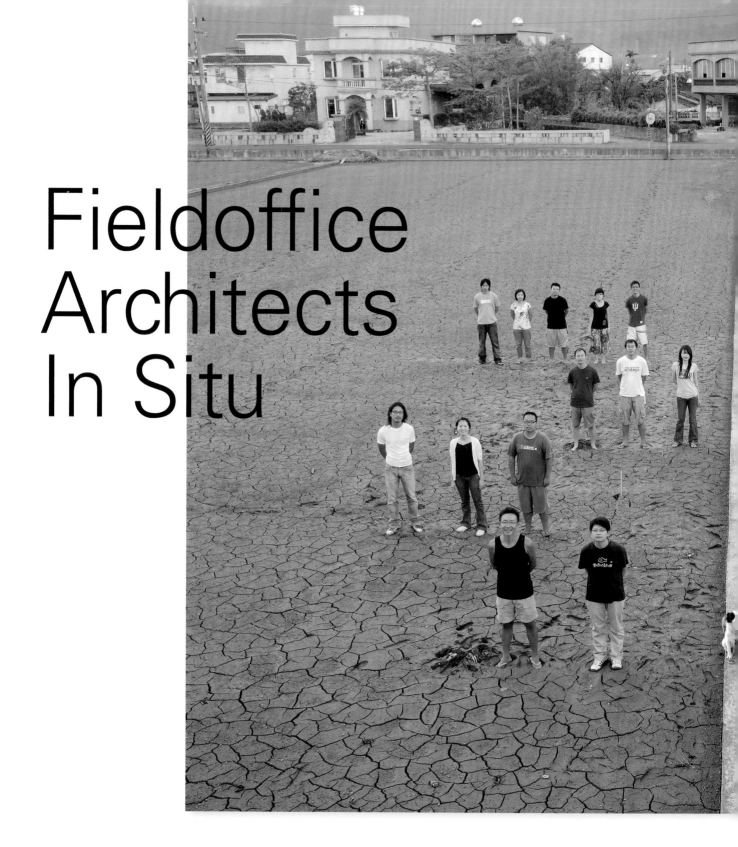

Fieldoffice Architects In Situ

Fieldoffice Architects,
City and Rural as a Family,
Yilan County,
Taiwan,
2010

Balancing the relationship between
rural and urban is a way of living in
the rural–urban mix, Yilan.

Sheng-Yuan Huang
and Yu-Hsiang Hung

Reflecting on the Rural–Urban Mix in Yilan, Taiwan

Yilan is generally considered a rural county with a city at its heart. Fieldoffice Architects, whose team live and work entirely in this area and are deeply immersed in its community, take a more holistic view. Their collaborative approach blurs the boundaries between rural and urban, with architecture and environmental design projects interconnecting to form part of a regional framework. Principal **Sheng-Yuan Huang** and Project Architect **Yu-Hsiang Hung** reflect on their practice.

To be honest, I can barely distinguish the difference between the city region and the rural area of Yilan. Due to the small size of this territory, I can swim in the pond nearby the field. Then, I catch up with my colleagues in the breakfast shop in the city, on my way to the office in thirty minutes.
— Sheng-Yuan Huang, *Living in Place*, 2015[1]

The distinction between the city and the countryside is becoming increasingly blurred. For Fieldoffice Architects this condition is epitomised by Yilan, the location of our practice in northeastern Taiwan. An alliance of shared intent and a constantly expanding community, the office has grown to 30 people since it was set up in 1994. Yilan, a county embedded in an agricultural landscape, is only an hour's journey away from Taiwan's capital of Taipei City. It is conventionally perceived as a rural area but Fieldoffice see Yilan as a combination of rural and urban. The city now demands more of the rural area because of the increasing awareness of environmentalism,[2] and because of an appreciation of the elements of the mountains, sea and streams that define life in Yilan. The rural in Yilan is no longer the residual of the city: it complements the city in a reciprocal way.

The architects wish to assimilate themselves in the region and the local way of life with integrity. This enables them to stimulate an intimate and coherent relationship between their design and factors such as the constantly changing environment.[3] All of Fieldoffice's projects overlap one another, and are in a continual state of progression and revision.

Instead of proposing rigorous strategies for Yilan, the practice attempts to tell its story through four 'reflections' on the rural–urban mix of Yilan. These shared, guiding attitudes have both inspired our success and helped us through difficulties over the years.

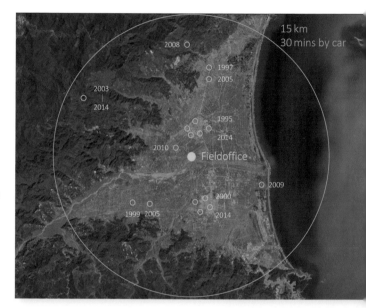

Fieldoffice Architects,
Projects Map,
Yilan County,
Taiwan,
2015

The office is in the centre of Langtang Delta; the projects in Yilan territory can be reached by car within 30 minutes.

Fieldoffice Architects,
Yilan City-Rural,
Yilan County,
Taiwan,
2015

Yilan comprises both city and rural geographic features, shaping the territory as a city–rural model.

Reflecting on 'Time as a Friend'

It is a story of a young man inspired by the unique climate condition, geography and rebellious spirits of this territory; he has slowly realised that Taiwan's democratic nature has always been very much alive, that the young generation is free from the restraints of conventions and adaptable to the ever-changing social and cultural environment.
— Fieldoffice Architects and Sheng-Yuan Huang, *Living in Place*, 2015[4]

The core of each project does not correspond merely to a single architectural construction, but also to time: a project does not end at its physical completion. Taking the Yilan Old Town Promenade Project as an example, our intervention was to introduce open spaces between the neighbourhoods and the public institutions in the corridor that runs towards the riverside. This provided an opportunity to slow down the privatisation of land next to the riverbank, and we inserted the Yilan Social Welfare Centre in the corridor, with a courtyard corresponding to its urban environment.

The project has taken several years and has required patience, and began with an invitation to all kinds of participants to express their views. Local inhabitants formed their own networks to connect one another. A mutual trust has been established over time between our studio and the locals. Using this foundation, Fieldoffice Architects gradually explored and teased out a diversity of design alternatives for civil infrastructure and bridge construction, including continuing the promenade across the Yilan River. When our project is utilised and enjoyed the design is effectively still in progress, for life itself is part of the design concept.

Our approach encourages the younger generation of architects to search freely for their own clients, to seek out different resources and to work in a spirit of collaboration. Over a long time span, this has helped to broaden our focus from a single type of architectural project in the city to a regional framework that includes the 'rural' areas.

Fieldoffice Architects,
Yilan Social Welfare Centre, Yilan City,
Taiwan,
2001

above: The Yilan Social Welfare Centre is an anchored social space in the corridor that runs towards the riverside and connects public spaces.

Fieldoffice Architects,
Jin-Mei Parasitic Pathway,
Yilan City,
Taiwan,
2008

above middle: The locals are familiar with the tectonics of this attached structure and make use of it in their own way.

right: An alternative pathway is attached underneath the existing bridge, continuing the corridor across the Yilan River.

Reflecting on 'The Sheltering Capacity of the Urban-Field Canopy'

> Echoing with the play of light and shadow generated from the huge abstract canopy underneath, this datum can effectively depict its position within the surrounding 'urban-field' context.
> — Fieldoffice Architects, 'Exhibition info – Fieldoffice: Living in Place', 2015[5]

For a long time, the washing-shed has been a common structure in the agricultural areas of Yilan. It is an important archetype in the region because it protects people from the rainy climate and acts as a gathering place for human activities and interaction. In this sense, this shed can be perceived as a mediator between the built environment and the rural area.

The Luodong Cultural Working House, in the rainy subtropical zone of Yilan, is a transformation of the washing-shed archetype. It reveals the beauty of the familiar landscape to the public eye while protecting the rural elements underneath, such as the irrigating streams and fields. The canopy frame of the Luodong Cultural Working House ostensibly has a sheltering function and it was also a budget-friendly solution.[6] For us, its real function is consciously to 'create emptiness', which spatially emphasises that it is a democratic, boundary-blurring, classless space, while also expressing the vitality of the rural.

This emptiness anticipates the venue's public common use as an urban amenity. While it makes a pronounced statement through its form, it also serves as a backdrop for various social activities. The flow of the public on the ground gives the place its purpose and identity. The canopy dissolves the boundary between the city and rural, inviting everyone into this urban-field, and anticipates the future development of the surrounding regions.

Fieldoffice Architects,
Luodong Cultural Working House,
Loudong Township,
2014

The canopy dissolves the boundary between the city and the rural, inviting people to this urban-field.

Washing-shed,
Yilan County,
Taiwan

For years, the washing-shed has been a critical archetype in Yilan territory, sheltering people undertaking agricultural work in the countryside.

Washing-shed,
Yilan County,
Taiwan

For years, the washing-shed has been a critical archetype in Yilan territory, sheltering people undertaking agricultural work in the countryside.

Reflecting on 'Learning from the Delta, Water and Territory'

In retrospect we discovered that a city cannot enjoy long prosperity if it only cared about itself, because the breezes, the water and the ecosystem have to retain their vitality after passing through the city. The urban and the rural have to not only help each other but also coexist upon each other, in which creative governance can also be inspired from this reciprocal way.
— Fieldoffice Architects and Sheng-Yuan Huang,
Living in Place, 2015[7]

Fieldoffice Architects,
The Boat,
Yilan County,
Taiwan,
2012

The architects built a boat in order to have a better understanding of the infrastructural elements of the waterways.

In 2003, Fieldoffice Architects decided to move out of Yilan city and settled at its border so that we could travel between the city and rural areas more freely. We have learned how to cultivate rice in paddy fields, to experience swimming alongside the road, to cook for ourselves and even to build our own boats for a better understanding of the waterways. The purpose of all these exercises is to bring healthier living to our 'family'. The idea of the Fieldoffice Architecture School is to encourage more young people to use rural infrastructural elements such as waterways, and in the process learn how to protect them. Manipulating infrastructures is then directed toward the 'irrigation of territories with potential',[8] sowing the seeds of future possibilities.

A few years later, through the 'landscape lavatory', the 'water pump station', the 'war memorial' and other environmental design projects, we repeatedly investigated the dynamic systems of the Lanyang Delta. We wanted to discover how the river affects every part of the city and the rural area. Seeing our determination, people from different fields began voluntarily to share their expertise until we had acquired the necessary working knowledge. A full, long-term understanding of the delta and the relationship between the city and the rural has enabled us to project new possibilities for the future.

Fieldoffice Architects,
The Dormitory of Fieldoffice,
Yilan County,
Taiwan,
2012

Fieldoffice Architects settled on the border between the city and the rural area in 2003.

Final Reflections on 'Living in the Rural-Urban Mix, Yilan'

I hope everyone has a chance to strive for the beauty of his or her own homeland.
— Sheng-Yuan Huang, *Living in Place*, 2015[9]

Following surveys of local transportation and flood regulation systems of the city region and the countryside of Yilan, we were finally given the opportunity to rebuild the 'new moat' in Yilan city. This cross-disciplinary venture helps flood control in the countryside, as well as connecting to the historical sense of the city centre.

We believe that long-term disaster prevention, economic stability and industrial security form the foundation for a good life. In this sense, the rural area is an inseparable part of city-making. Only from the basis of having stable homes and relationships with people can we then protect our environment for as long as possible. ᴆ

Notes
1. Fieldoffice Architects and Sheng-Yuan Huang, *Living in Place*, TOTO Publishing (Tokyo), 2015, pp 28–9.
2. James Corner, 'Chapter 1: Terra Fluxus', in *Landscape Urbanism Reader*, Princeton Architectural Press (New York), 2006, pp 23–32.
3. Sheng-Yuan Huang, *Fieldoffice Architects + Introduction in East Asian Society Symposium*, Chung-Yuan Christian University Department of Architecture (Taichung), 2014, p 73.
4. Fieldoffice Architects and Sheng-Yuan Huang, *Living in Place*, op. cit., p 31.
5. Fieldoffice Architects, 'Exhibition info – Fieldoffice: Living in Place', accessed 8 December 2015: http://www.fieldoffice-architects.com/toto-gallery-ma-exhibition-living-in-place-tokyo-japan-7-10-9-12-2015.
6. Shih-Wei Lo, *Agitating Border: A Review of Huang Sheng-Yuan's, Chiu Wen-Chieh (Da-han)'s and Lu Li-Hwang (Interbreeding Field)'s Locally Constructing Through Deleuzean and Bataillean Viewpoints*, Research Centre of Architecture and Urbanism THU (Taichung), 2006, pp 45–7.
7. Fieldoffice Architects and Sheng-Yuan Huang, *Living in Place*, op. cit., p 139.
8. Rem Koolhaas and Bruce Mau, 'Whatever Happened to Urbanism?', *S,M,L,XL*, Monacelli Press (New York), 1995, p 969.
9. Sheng-Yuan Huang and Fieldoffice Architects, *Living in Place*, op. cit., pp 276–7.

Fieldoffice Architects,
New City Moat,
Yilan City,
Taiwan,
2010–

The cross-disciplinary venture combines flood control and historical references.

The rural area is an inseparable part of city-making. Only from the basis of having stable homes and relationships with people can we then protect our environment for as long as possible.

In the Hands of the People

Harnessing the Collective Power of Village Life in India

Top-down attempts by governments and charities to rebuild rural communities after natural disasters, or to rehabilitate slums, can leave communities feeling fractured. The Hunnarshala Foundation instead focuses on re-establishing social capital, providing funding and professional support for residents so that they can work together to improve their lot. This also reinforces the value of traditional artisans' knowledge in solving modern problems. Hunnarshala's Executive Vice Chairman **Sandeep Virmani** explains.

In 1987 I was a young architect on fellowship to study rural architecture. This was an Indo-German initiative to allow professionals like me to find relevance for their skills in service. I had chosen to help a small farm labour community of Vankars (a weaver caste) in South Gujarat in western India build their homes. The 127 families would meet every morning from 4am until daybreak at 7am to collectively labour and give shape to their new village. Afterwards they left to work on the farms of other communities to earn their daily wage. Since that time I have witnessed this time and time again.

Recently when I visited Bhutan in the Himalayas, I woke early to make my way through the fog in the Phobjikha valley, looking for the white-necked cranes who had descended from Tibet. A faint sound of a song with thumping sounds led me to a rammed-earth house being built with the 12 to 15 men and women pounding their rammers in unison to the song's tune. They had collected to help a widow make her home, while she prepared some butter tea and Ema Datsi (a traditional dish of chillis and cheese) for the guests.

In Kutch, in the Banni region of Gujarat where the pastorals graze, they have a name for this activity. They call it 'Aabhat'; a practice where members of a community pull together their labour for the benefit of all and/or the weak in the community. They make homes, wells, clear grasslands of bush and so on. But it always ends with eating together and sharing the positive energy of having achieved a task that strengthens their trust in one another and gives them the opportunity to serve.

This is a 'rural' value that exists all over the Eastern world and was prevalent everywhere only a century ago. The social capital that rural communities harness is based on the existence of informal values or norms shared among members of a group that permit cooperation among them.[1]

Hunnarshala Foundation, Post-flood rehabilitation, Bihar, India, 2008

previous spread: The bamboo workers of the Mithila region collaborated with Hunnarshala and the Owner Driven Reconstruction Collaborative (ODRC), a collection of NGOs and private individuals, to design this prefabricated home. The house was built using only one tool, a *dabia* (a machete to cut and shape bamboo). The bamboo wattle was then plastered with earth on the inside and cement on the outside. Hunnarshala and the ODRC helped the state government to develop the policy and technical guidelines for the Bihar rehabilitation scheme, provided training, and assisted in the implementation of the programme.

Hunnarshala Foundation, Post-tsunami reconstruction, Aceh, Sumatra, Indonesia, 2004

below left: The Hunnarshala Foundation and Uplink (Indonesian NGOs) helped the *Panglima Laut* (leader) of this lagoon fishing community of 23 villages build 3,500 homes.

below right: Traditional stilted homes kept families safe from sea surges. This adaptation replaces wooden columns with reinforced cement concrete (RCC), with a light wooden first storey to withstand both earthquakes and sea surges.

Housing: An Opportunity to Build Social Capital

This trust can achieve seemingly impossible feats. In 2004 in Aceh, on the eastern tip of Sumatra, Indonesia, the tsunami completely wiped out all recognisable features of property holding. The land records were destroyed as well, leaving no tangible 'proof' to re-establish property rights. The India-based Hunnarshala Foundation along with Uplink (a group of Indonesian NGOs) suggested the *Panglima Laut*, the head man of a lagoon of 23 fishing community villages, form a committee of trusted individuals, and as they placed sticks to mark the properties of the owners, we used the recently developed technology of a Total Station Survey (TSS) machine to create maps of the sites. Under Islam, a proposal placed in the public domain is open to correction for a week, after which it is considered adopted in the 'presence of God'. Within a few months, more than 5,000 properties were re-established using this system of trust and social norm – supported with technology.

Contrary to modern values of self-realisation through self-serving ambition, many rural regions strive to self-actualise through actions of public good. To allow for such trust norms in communities to play out, it is necessary to have faith in the innate human spirit that is realised when they reach out to others. The Hunnarshala Foundation's housing reconstruction programmes are therefore structured so as to be in the hands of the people; unlike most programmes where governments or charities build the homes that are then handed over to the people, Hunnarshala gives the assistance money to owners to design and build their homes, and provides support from professionals including social workers, designers and construction supervisors. This approach allows communities to make collective decisions, encouraging trust among them. The weekly or fortnightly meeting of stakeholders is

considered sacrosanct and a place of reverence; a place for opportunities to create social capital, for creativity and solving disputes in the spirit of giving, all using the housing programme as a medium and not just an end. In the Kutch district of Gujarat, for example, after the earthquake of 2001, in one such meeting a Meghwal masons community we worked with put a moratorium on any masons leaving the village until their own village was completed. They also decided on a common wage (lower than market price) for all skilled and unskilled labour, reasoning that engagement in rebuilding their lives held greater premium than skills in the market.

In Bihar in East India, after the 2008 Kosi floods, Hunnarshala undertook a participatory rehabilitation exercise on behalf of the state government. Many of the local people did not possess homestead land, and the government could only provide home plots far away from their community. The community therefore requested that instead of land, the government provide the financial assistance for 5 *dhur* (44 square metres/474 square feet) to the landless to acquire land of their choice on which to build their homes. A further condition was that construction of the Tola (hamlet) could not begin until everyone in the community had homestead land. This put pressure on the residents to ensure that the necessary arrangements were in place for the landless among them to purchase land in the Tola. As a result, many shared their land with the landless even though the money they received was much less than the market price of the land they gave away.

Hunnarshala Foundation, Earthquake reconstruction, Kutch district, Gujarat, India, 2001

below bottom: The traditional circular homes (*bhunga*) of pastoral communities in Kutch have an arch action in the lateral thrusts of an earthquake that prevents them from breaking. This was introduced after the 1819 earthquake by the Meghwal people. Post-earthquake in 2001, Hunnarshala helped them redesign the *bhunga* with stabilised earth walls and an octagonal tiled roof.

Hunnarshala Foundation, Slum rehabilitation, Bhuj, Kutch district, Gujarat, India, 2015

below left: India has set an ambitious target to build 20 million homes for the urban poor by 2022. As part of a community-driven approach, Hunnarshala has begun building 300 of 12,000 homes with the Bhuj municipality to make the city slum free. Each slum dweller is provided with 65 square metres (700 square feet) of land and financial assistance.

The ability of rural communities to place trust in the group for the wider good is also exemplified when they bring this rurality into the cities and live in slums. In Hunnarshala's recent rehabilitation project in the city of Bhuj in the Kutch district, the slum communities have organised the layout of their neighbourhood in sub-clusters of 8 to 15 homes, avoiding compound walls and instead bringing their private spaces into the community realm. They have collectively procured materials for construction and recycled those from their earlier shacks, and used their own labour to build homes with 30 per cent more space than the government/developer-built housing for the same cost. As the group builds together, they take responsibility for building for the infirm, single and elderly.

Unfortunately, urban sensibility does not allow communities to develop. We have relinquished this important social construct to real-estate developers. Neighbours are now determined based on affordability of homes, dividing the city along lines of class. This has many negative connotations, for example denying our children the potential of learning about difference, slowly creating a mistrust and fear of the poor and vice versa. Further, little understanding of our neighbours results in an inability to govern our neighbourhoods, and the relinquishing of this control of our lives to municipal corporations whom we do not trust either.

In Hunnarshala's slum rehabilitation programmes in Bhuj, the self-governing nature of such communities encouraged the Foundation and the municipality to consider developing a taxation policy whereby neighbourhoods will be given rebates for managing their own water, sewerage and garbage. A pilot project was therefore proposed in order to test and understand how the technologies and management systems would be developed by the Resident Welfare Association under such a scheme, Ramdev Nagar, a rehab neighbourhood of 116 homes, will recharge their aquifer, pump and supply water to all households, ration water based on availability in their aquifer, treat and recycle the grey water for flushing and planting trees, and manage a zero-waste centre for garbage, which will be segregated for reuse.

Artisans as Knowledge Bearers

Only two hours from Delhi, in a small village in the Shamli district of western Uttar Pradesh, Nawab introduces me to his *Ustad* (teacher), Mistri Yaseen. A communal riot victim struggling to put his life back together. Hunnarshala is helping Nawab and 150 families to build their new villages after the 2013 Hindu–Muslim clash that left thousands of muslims homeless. His *Ustad* is an old diminutive man with a bent back, but proudly says that Nawab was his best student. Nawab is the youngest in line of a 400-year-old tradition that has passed down the skills and knowledge of building *Daat Chat* (shallow dome) roofs. Sitting on top of one such dome, Nawab explains that this roof is cheaper and stronger than any made from reinforced cement concrete (RCC) because it is constructed of a homogeneous material of bricks: 'RCC tries to marry steel and cement, and sooner or later they will want to divorce.'

We are living in times where we struggle to find solutions to the destructive practice of high energy-use, carbon emissions, excessive building and lifestyles. However, technologies developed by rural artisans are offering us the knowledge, skills

and sensibility that have sustained this world for centuries. Shallow domes can replace roof slabs that typically account for 20 per cent of the total cement and 70 to 75 per cent of steel used in load-bearing structures, drastically reducing carbon emissions. Further, they are 20 to 30 per cent cheaper with longer life spans than RCC. Nawab is now involved in a research project being undertaken by Gram Vidya (a building research organisation in Bangalore) and the Hunnarshala Foundation to investigate how shallow domes might replace RCC in mass housing programmes in India.

A second important value that rurality brings to us all is the ability of rural societies to nurture and build upon centuries-old knowledge. In Hunnarshala's projects, master artisans like Nawab are given the stature, place and opportunity to engage with and provide solutions to modern problems. Modern construction chains have relegated rural artisans to the role of only implementing the visions of architects and builders on construction sites, stifling their knowledge. But their ability to use hands, heart and mind to create can provide solutions that are simple and efficient.

Hunnarshala Foundation,
Rehabilitation
of riot victims,
Shamli,
Uttar Pradesh,
India,
2014

This 400-year-old shallow dome construction technique has become very popular with architects and researchers since it was documented on Hunnarshala's website. Hunnarshala is now supporting the formation of a company of masons to cater to demand from across the country.

Inverted Ceiling Montage

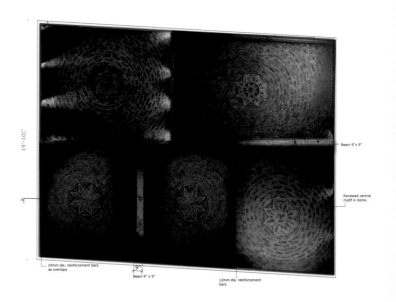

Technologies developed by rural artisans are offering us the knowledge, skills and sensibility that have sustained this world for centuries.

Artisans are not merely technical professionals, like their counterparts in urban societies – they decide on how technology shapes societal values in rural cultures that give high premium to the simplicity and frugality of their lifestyle.

For example, along with a hundred colleagues from two villages in Madhya Pradesh, Ramesh came to Kutch as migrant labour seeking work post-earthquake in 2001. During the rehabilitation work Hunnarshala realised these workers had excellent knowledge of earth-based construction: they had built their own homes with earth back in their farming communities. Though earth is a complex material, without technical tests they were able to decide on the appropriate physical attributes of sand, silt and clay mixtures for walls, and even decipher salinity and alkalinity in soils. Ramesh today runs a successful company providing earth walling services with an annual turnover of up to 2 million rupees (US$30,000). With his colleagues he has worked on prestigious UNESCO buildings in Abu Dhabi, and trained insurgent returnees in Aceh, Indonesia, setting up stabilised earth block production enterprises. He also contributes a part

Hunnarshala Foundation, Restoration of Al Jahili Fort, Al Ain, Abu Dhabi, United Arab Emirates, 2009

below top: Hunnarshala earth artisans restored this UNESCO-accredited fort, Al Jahili in Al Ain.

Hunnarshala Foundation office, Bhuj, Kutch district, Gujarat, India, 2012

below bottom: Artisan companies supported by Hunnarshala build for the best architects in India. This office for Hunnarshala uses a variety of upgraded rural technologies such as adobe, wattle-and-daub and rammed-earth walls, thatch, recycled wood and earth for roofs and floors, and shallow domes.

of his income every year to a school that teaches young artisans in Hunnarshala. He sees this financial contribution as his social responsibility now that he is doing well.

Balancing Process and Product

The design of rural homes, though often simple in appearance, embodies more than meets the eye; they possess the tangible attributes of using local materials and consequently have low carbon footprints. However, it is the intangible, the process of building itself, which creates societies and is given equal importance in the rural communities illustrated here. These are human values that the urban has forsaken only in the last century and our rural is in danger of losing in the coming decades. But in the East we have a choice: to recapture these spiritual constructs within the human spirit by giving dignity to the rural artisan and once again building social capital. ᴅ

Note
1. Francis Fukuyama, 'Social Capital', The Tanner Lectures on Human Values, Brasenose College, Oxford 1997, p 378: http://tannerlectures. utah.edu/_documents/a-to-z/f/Fukuyama98.pdf.

John Lin

Designing
for an
Uncertain
Future

Rural Urban Framework,
Shichuang Village House
Prototype, Guangdong
Province, China

Recent decades in rural China have seen a dramatic shift from traditional courtyard houses that could be extended horizontally, to standardised concrete-frame constructions on limited plots that can grow only upwards. As the rural–urban divide disintegrates, the rural needs to be redefined. Guest-Editor **John Lin** of Rural Urban Framework outlines the practice's proposals for a vertical core that could utilise government subsidies to offer a more diverse, flexible development model for village life.

Rural Urban Framework (RUF),
Shichuang Village House Prototype,
Guangdong Province,
China,
2015

left: Aerial view of Shichuang Village with the community centre designed by RUF in front. The centre is used for weddings, funerals and other important events. Though the village is often empty, the community centre stages large events when villagers come home.

above: Aerial view of Shichuang Village. In the 1990s, the government froze the boundary of land allocated for building new houses, driving the village to expand vertically.

Chinese villages are the real frontline in the country's urbanisation process. Over the past 30 years, even though rural migrants have enabled the construction of China's cities, it is estimated that the total amount of rural construction currently far exceeds that of the urban. Built with remittances sent home, on limited plots of land reserved for house construction, the rural village comes to quickly resemble an urban village. In the process, the rural economy has become entirely dependent on the city. Paradoxically, this cycle of migration and construction leads to increasingly dense villages with gradually emptying populations. The image of a timeless pastoral existence is replaced by an incomplete urbanity. Neither rural nor urban, these villages exist in a state of uncertainty. As the relationship between the rural and the urban continues to evolve while also remaining interdependent, the rural is open to new definition.

Dissolving the Rural–Urban Divide

In the near future, this is all set to change. Two main government policies that have so far enabled the current urban economic expansion are the *hukou* (household registration policy) and the collective land-use rights of villagers. In the past, the *hukou* upheld that citizens be classified as either rural or urban, which determined their eligibility to receive education and healthcare benefits. In maintaining this rural–urban divide, but simultaneously releasing villagers from collective agricultural production, these policies effectively created an enormous migrant workforce, while also preventing workers from permanently settling down in cities. However, in cities such as Xiamen, the government is now experimenting with measures that begin to allow the slow integration of rural migrants through changes to their *hukou* status based on an established points system.

In order to prevent the flood of migrants into the city, this easing of *hukou* restrictions is counterbalanced by reforms to the collective land-use policies. In Chengdu in western China, programmes such as the Rural Equities Exchange encourage the transfer of land-management rights between villagers and investors. By creating a platform for these exchanges to take place that makes the process more transparent and accountable, the hope is to stimulate the rural economy through the leasing of land. The first stage of this process opens up restraints on the use of collective land rights, while in future it is anticipated that villagers will be able to utilise individual house-building land, leasing their own plots or houses for economic purposes. In effect this will introduce commercial programmes into the village fabric, further speeding up the transition from rural to urban.

In the 1950s Chairman Mao established the *hukou* policy and the collectivisation of farming, fundamentals of the rural–urban divide. But later, in 1978, the economic reform instigated by Deng Xiaoping began to incrementally dissolve this. If the first step of economic reform was the construction of cities made possible through migrant labour, then the new task is the reconstruction of the countryside. As villages lose their collective identity, how can we address this and other consequences of rural urbanisation through design?

From Houses to Housing

In 2014, in the village of Shichuang outside of Guangzhou in Guangdong Province, Rural Urban Framework (RUF) experimented with flexible housing prototypes that began to anticipate the shifts in government policy and respond to the current conditions of growth and resulting social and economic transformation of this rural community by adapting to the individual and changing needs of the villagers.

The project was initiated as the result of the desire of the village head to build a new house for himself and his brother on two adjacent plots of land. By combining the two plots for a single house shared by two families, his hope was to maximise the use of the land. RUF recognised this as a moment of transition from single village houses to collective housing. The prototype design therefore envisioned a shared core of programmes and added communal spaces, with potential future shops on the ground floor. Though the proposal was not realised (the family in the end opted to simply build two adjoining houses), the concept of the core remained.

Le Corbusier Maison Dom-ino-style construction in China. This system of construction transforms all possible programmes (houses, schools, hospitals) into a single generic building type.

Interior of a modern village house. Most of the evidence of the previous agricultural-based lifestyle is gone.

As villages lose their collective identity, how can we address this and other consequences of rural urbanisation through design?

Plan of Shichuang Village. The village is a mixture of traditional courtyard houses and three- to four-storey concrete-frame houses.

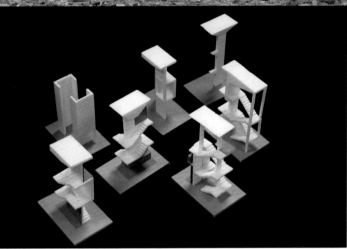

Models of new village house cores proposed by RUF. The core can be built for 40,000 yuan, the equivalent of the government subsidy.

Recent changes in landownership, densification and social transformation have created new strategies for dividing, sharing and allocating living units in rural China. The traditional Chinese courtyard house was once a system that exemplified not only the necessities of agricultural life, but a clear social organisation that also provided the means for expansion and growth. From a single courtyard, the house would expand outwards, adding further courtyards and eventually accommodating upwards of 100 families – a single ancestral house could become an entire village. But with economic reforms came a new style of house construction, a concrete post and slab construction with infill brick walls, easily adaptable to any requirement. The power of this building type was exemplified by Le Corbusier in his Maison Dom-ino (1914–15). In the 1990s the government began to freeze the boundary of land allocated for house construction in the countryside. Contained within a single collective plot and combined with the new concrete frame system, this drove Chinese villages to expand upwards. Typically built as a standard three- to four-storey generic model, some villages near Guangzhou have now reached 10 to 12 storeys. The current system of house construction has thus shifted dramatically from horizontal to vertical growth.

Le Corbusier anticipated that this system of construction would lead to freedom in adaptation and variation. However, because of the tendency to hire outside contractors to build these houses while villagers migrate to the cities in search of work, they are surprisingly uniform. Rooms are standard size, often ending up empty or too cramped. The remains of agricultural production such as food drying, the smoking of meats, milling grain and other social activities once well situated in the courtyard are moved inside. As the right to build a village house is passed along the lineage of sons, brothers increasingly have to share a single house. The village is no longer a collection of singular houses, but increasingly a system of collective housing – an urban typology without the diversity of urban life.

The village is no longer a collection of singular houses, but increasingly a system of collective housing – an urban typology without the diversity of urban life.

A Flexible Prototype

Shichuang Village is currently in the midst of a building boom. A government programme established in 2010 grants a 40,000-yuan subsidy for each villager to tear down their remaining mud-brick courtyard houses and build multistorey concrete-frame ones in their place. In just six years, over half of the houses have been replaced. The subsidy is enough to build the initial floor of the house, leaving room for further expansion, which is funded separately by the villagers. RUF's alternative proposal, rather than utilising the government funding for a ground floor, imagines a three-storey vertical core that could lead to a new process of village house construction.

A series of core prototypes were developed that enable different scenarios for growth. These correspond to the villagers' current house-funding model in which floors are added as money becomes available. The village therefore grows at different speeds: by investing in the house as an incremental process, it can take up to 20 years to complete. RUF's strategic model thus allows for half-finished or incomplete houses to incorporate the recycling of old materials from the traditional house, retain an open courtyard space for commercial and communal activities, and have a rooftop garden, with water storage and recycling implemented within the vertical core. There is space for household planting, as well as entrepreneurial activities. The village is therefore a congestion of building varieties and social interaction, rather than the current model of uniformity. As the incomes and lifestyles of the villagers diversify, their village can begin to express the best of these urban qualities.

RUF's design strategies for vertical-core collective housing try to situate the relationship between control and freedom. Whether at the scale of a building or a village, the design of a more specific core enables greater use of the house plot in its incremental stages. Instead of determining a final outcome, as Shichuang Village inevitably transforms into a microcosm of urban life, RUF's attempts to create a balance between the collective and the individual embrace the possibility of uncertainty.

China's villages are facing a renaissance. As industrial methods take over, they will no longer be constrained by agricultural production. Where Chairman Mao previously set up the rural–urban divide to complement industrial and agricultural production, the new China is beginning to rely on the rural as an economic driver. This completes and transforms Deng's vision of migrant labour as a rising consumer class. But many questions remain. Even though the one-child policy has ended, its effects are ongoing. Can the resulting increasing level of dependency on one child supporting two parents and raising multiple children be utilised to revitalise the villages? Will the economic benefits of individual land-use rights counterbalance the easing of *hukou* restrictions? Will villagers continue to rush to the cities? One certainty remains: rural villages continue to be at the frontline of future development in China, and as the rural–urban divide gradually disappears it is even more important for the rural to redefine itself both spatially and conceptually. ∆

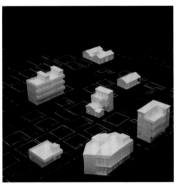 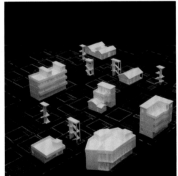 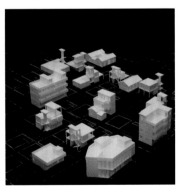

Models showing the insertion of the RUF-designed cores, demonstrating alternative scenarios for future village development.

Rural villages continue to be at the frontline of future development in China

Anders Abraham and
Christina Capetillo

The Hunstad Code

Anders Abraham and
Christina Capetillo,
Hunstad,
Sweden,
2008–11

A birch wood close to the
site of Hunstad.

With modern technology
and levels of prosperity
making many of us
increasingly self-sufficient,
architects **Anders Abraham
and Christina Capetillo**
argue that a rural 'town'
is defined by the level of
interactivity within it rather
than merely by population
figures. In collaboration
with curators Annesofie
Becker and Martin
Christiansen, they have
developed the Hunstad
Code to offer guidelines
for the construction of
environments that can
encourage the development
of relationships between
residents even while
remaining low-density.

Rules for the Planning of a Rural Town

Hunstad is an architectural project that raises questions about space and urbanity – about how we imagine a town and its creation. It asks when a settlement is a rural town, a satellite town or a suburb. When are you a citizen, a visitor or merely a stranger among strangers? Commissioned by the Danish Arts Foundation, it is a planned rural town on the outskirts of Brösarp, a small community of 680 inhabitants, about 100 kilometres (62 miles) northeast of Malmö.

This southern part of Sweden is characterised by the bigger cities of Malmö and Gothenburg, a long coastline along the Baltic Sea, and beautiful, undulating morainal landscapes, but also a series of smaller towns such as Brösarp, which in recent decades has suffered the effects of depopulation and recession. Local forces were therefore keen to devise initiatives to attract new activity to the area, both culturally and economically.

The Neon Gallery, which was located in Brösarp at the time, was interested in expanding its venue with the creation of an experimental rural town that would bring people to the area for longer periods than tourists and summer cottage guests. Housed in the workshop and warehouse buildings of the former 'road station', a storage and maintenance facility of the Swedish Road Administration from 1998, the Neon cultural venue for contemporary art, music, theatre and dance focused on the innovative and experimental within different art forms through its exhibitions, concerts, performances, workshops and seminars. The Hunstad project is based on the idea of developing a small rural town of 17 houses around this former cultural hub, to be used for study and work stays by artists, researchers, students, children and young people.

Hunstad is an architectural project that raises questions about space and urbanity

Anders Abraham and Christina Capetillo, Hunstad, Sweden, 2008–11

Site plan. It is not the town's houses as static objects but the relational whole that gives Hunstad an urban dimension.

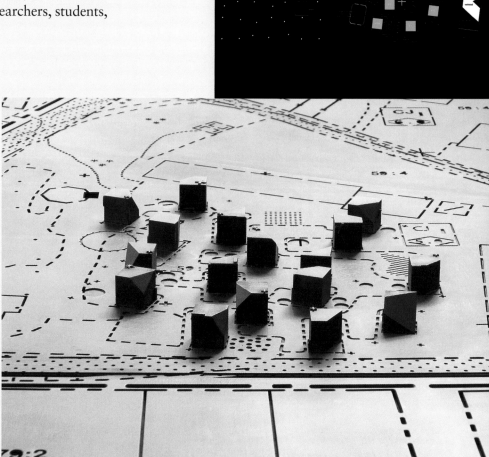

Site model. The Hunstad project raises the fundamental question: What does it take for somewhere to be a rural town?

All of Hunstad's 17 houses are different from each other, ranging from being homogeneous to heterogeneous.

Many houses simply stand alone, side by side, rather than identifying themselves with and becoming a part of the urbanity that connects and produces cohesion

A New Nature

Many would, in looking at this dense world of objects they see around them, see a new 'nature', which is just as irrational, incomprehensible and ruthless as the original nature.
— Willy Ørskov, *Objekterne – proces og tilstand. Forslag til en objektteori*, 1972[1]

Contemporary architecture often struggles to establish cohesion. When we design and construct buildings, naturally we enter an already existing context. Even so, many houses simply stand alone, side by side, rather than identifying themselves with and becoming a part of the urbanity that connects and produces cohesion in the culturally created – the 'new nature'. Architecture is a condition that builds on relations, because that which matters one day either loses its significance or means something else the next. The city is formed in the moment. What must therefore be central to our deliberations about urban development is that though we cannot retain the form, we can create spatial and social conditions instead.

Hunstad is based on the concept of the multifaceted, understood as the complex and changing context in which the relationship between the individual and the many is a constitutive problem forming both subject and object. By taking the diverse physical and programmatic organisations of the contemporary city as a point of departure and considering the culturally created as conditions, it becomes possible to formulate architectural ideas by building from what the world is made of.

The Hunstad Code describes the
rules for the development of the
new town.

The project raised an important fundamental question: What does it take for somewhere to be a rural town? To answer this, it was necessary to develop a set of new guidelines – alternative construction regulations for a sparsely populated urban condition (a village or a suburb) – as the aim of existing building codes was only to simplify, organise and separate instead of building relations and achieving the density required to generate an urban environment.

According to Statistics Denmark, a town is a place with more than 200 and less than 999 inhabitants.[2] After several trips to minor towns, it became clear that it was not the number of inhabitants, but rather how much was going on in the individual places that made them towns. The social interactions and 'dependency' that emerge through a number of basic programmes in a town – a school, shops, hairdresser – combine so that the houses form a small society that opens up and constitutes a space between the regional infrastructure and the private plot of land. Without these various functions, it is merely a densification of houses, maintained solely by commuters.

Hunstad was developed out of a general concept of reliance – a degree of interdependence among the residents that creates relational spaces between houses and people. It was important to develop an architecture consisting of a series of units that could be assembled into either simple or complex houses containing basic programmes that would generate possibilities for individual residents to participate in and contribute to a social community.

**HUNSTAD
BYGNINGSREGLEMENT**
Regler for en planlagt landsby

THE HUNSTAD CODE
Rules for the planning of a
Rural town

UDKAST

The future site of the new town of
Hunstad. The site was previously a
storage and maintenance facility of
the Swedish Road Administration.

Plan of House 17, which is constructed of 17 different elements.

Views inside Hunstad town.

It is not the town's houses as static objects that form the urban dimension in Hunstad, but the relational whole. For this reason, each of the 17 houses, though built using a common construction system and sharing the same simple programmes and basic services, is different from the others.

Hunstad is a planned rural town that is both a small and large space – one of limited extension, consisting of relatively few units. However, its formless and varied nature, and the organisation of the houses in a non-hierarchical field, gives it great richness and diversity.

The houses range from being homogeneous – composed of many identical types and sizes of building elements, to heterogeneous – of many different types and sizes of building elements. They have both a private and a public realm, and all are equipped with a programme that initiates an event or produces an activity in the rural town. For example, the resident in House 14 selects a piece of music every day from Neon's archive, which is played in the town at noon. House 17 is equipped with a big screen on the roof, and each day the resident produces the town's image, a photo or something similar, which is shown at 4 pm. House 5 serves as a bicycle repair shop, which is kept open by the resident one hour per day. House 1 is home to the Hunstad Collection; everybody donates an object, such as a photograph or recording, when they depart or move away from the town, and all artists-in-residence donate a work.

Anders Abraham and
Christina Capetillo,
Guangdong Village
Code workshop,
University of
Hong Kong,
2013

left: A space in the old village
in Guangdong province, from
which the Guangdong Village
Code was developed.

opposite: The new town has
lost all the urban qualities of the
traditional village.

*The Hunstad Code is a tool that was developed
to produce relationships between residents in
a small rural town. The smaller the town, the
harder it is to make it function as a community.*

Each house has a small garden with different types
of trees, bushes and flowers growing in circular holes cut
into the tarmac of the former road station. The largest
of these contain uniform planting, while wilder and
heterogeneous types are planted in the smallest circles.
The large trees are alien to Hunstad and remind one of
other landscapes and towns, while the smaller trees are
regional and growing wild. Further to the 17 houses,
shared facilities such as a greenhouse, outdoor stage,
wild garden and a courtyard are erected on the site.
Two fruit orchards are planted in the transition space
between Hunstad and the town of Brösarp.

The Hunstad Code is a tool that was developed to
produce relationships between residents in a small rural
town. The smaller the town, the harder it is to make it
function as a community. Increased prosperity over the
last 30 years has brought a greater degree of autonomy.
People now have the financial latitude to build houses
that have all the necessary service features incorporated
so there is no longer a need for a communal laundry or
bathhouse. And we can buy all the machines and tools
required to maintain our gardens and houses. The result
is that relationships between neighbours have begun to
disappear, a condition exacerbated by a sense of self-
sufficiency, resulting in the expansion of the private
domain. More and more houses are surrounded by tall
hedges and fences. But you cannot be both a part of a
town and at the same time cut yourself off from it. The
Hunstad Code does not try to make rules that repeat
from the past, but instead attempts to find new ways to
encourage relationships and co-dependency.

In 2013, we conducted a workshop at the University of Hong Kong with 50 architecture students and travelled to Guangdong province in China to visit a small village where the old houses were about to be demolished to make room for new and better housing. In many ways the village had a great public space. However, it was evident that as the new town replaced the traditional village, it became a grouping of houses with no embedded urbanity. This small community could thus be seen as a victim of prosperity as it was transformed from a village to a suburb. Our studies of the old village resulted in the development of the Guangdong Village Code, founded on our observations of the public space and transformed into rules to be used in future planning.

The formulation of a code lies before the form – it is a spatial and social condition. Unfortunately, the realisation of Hunstad's 17 houses was put on hold in 2011 as the general financial crisis in Sweden meant that the client was unable to receive funding for the project. However, though the Hunstad Code began as a model for how to create a community for a rural town in Sweden, it is not site specific. It can be developed in relation to local opportunities and limitations and used as an important tool and inspiration to build a town anywhere. ⌂

For more on the Hunstad Code and architecture as the organisation of conditions see: Anders Abraham, *A New Nature: 9 Architectural Conditions between Liquid and Solid*, Lars Müller (Zurich), 2015. Selected models of Hunstad will be included at the 15th International Architecture Biennale in Venice, in the exhibition 'The Art of Many' at the Danish Pavilion (28 May to 27 November 2016).

Anders Abraham and Christina Capetillo,
Hunstad,
Sweden,
2008–11

Segment of the Hunstad site model (scale 1:20) showing the spaces between the houses of different complexities. Trees and greenery are planted in circular holes cut in the existing tarmac.

Notes
1. Willy Ørskov, *Objekterne – proces og tilstand. Forslag til en objektteori*, Borgen (Odense), 1972, p 10.
2. See: www.dst.dk/en/Statistik/dokumentation/documentationofstatistics/urban-areas-1--january/statistical-presentation.

The Hunstad Code can be developed in relation to local opportunities and limitations and used as an important tool and inspiration to build a town anywhere.

The Villages

Florida

1989–

Map of The Villages. The Villages is characterised by an infrastructural landscape of leisure, combined with a texture of detached 'single-family' houses, that is rolled out across vast areas of scraped-off ground.

Small-town Metropolitanism and the 'Middle of Nowhere'

With over 110,000 inhabitants, The Villages is the world's largest retirement community. Its numerous distinct 'villages', surrounded by artificial landscaping and golf courses and served by three 'downtowns', cater to those who crave the idealised rural life of times gone by while also offering the convenience and stimulation of the modern metropolis. **Deane Simpson**, leader of the Master's programme in Urbanism and Societal Change at the Royal Danish Academy of Fine Arts School of Architecture, investigates.

At the intersection of demographic ageing on the one hand, and the development logics of late-capitalism on the other, The Villages is an experiment in scalar elasticity – realising a settlement that functions simultaneously as a 'village' in the countryside and as a metropolitan centre for the young-old.

Located in the hinterland of Central Florida midway between the cities of Orlando and Ocala, the largest retirement community in the world is a privately developed lifestyle product for the over-55 'active adult' age group. It accommodates an estimated 114,350 inhabitants, articulating a new scale of demographically segregated 'dropout enclave'.[1] Envisioned by its founders as a 'Disney World for Active Retirees',[2] The Villages both emulates and expands upon the dominant model of postwar American retirement urbanism originated in Del Webb's Sun City of the early 1960s. Central to The Villages' emulation of Sun City is the interpretation of the countryside as a form of tabula rasa – a predominantly characterless ground upon which the development protocols of the 'active adult' community as a spatial product are 'rolled out'. The particularities and character of the setting, on the other hand, are defined at a larger scale, through the potentiality of its favourable climatic conditions and its proximity to road and airport infrastructure.

The themed downtowns, such as Spanish Springs Town Square shown here, contain a carefully curated range of objects and street furniture intended to communicate historical small-town America.

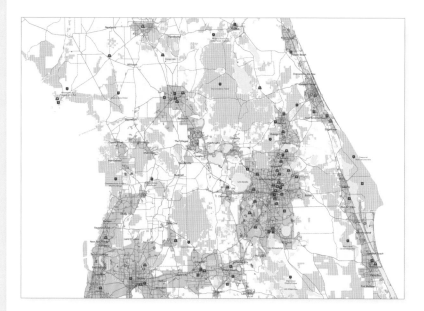

The location of Orange Blossom Gardens in the early 1980s was both in the 'middle of nowhere' and exhibited favourable infrastructural connectivity and climatic conditions, especially during the winter months.

Indicated on the map with the red outline between Orlando and Ocala, The Villages has grown to become the largest retirement community in the world.

From Orange Blossom Gardens to The Villages

The Villages emerged from what was, prior to 1989, known as Orange Blossom Gardens, a mobile home (trailer) park of nearly 400 homes built upon pumpkin fields and horse grazing land in the 1970s and early 1980s.[3] The vision for the park changed with the visit of owner Harold Schwartz in the early 1980s to his sister Ethel Shaw in Sun City, Arizona.[4] Schwartz was reportedly impressed by the scale and quality of Sun City, and particularly its ability to attract residents based on selling a 'lifestyle' rather than a specific quality intrinsically related to its physical setting, landscape or location. As was the case with Sun City, the location of Orange Blossom Gardens in the early 1980s was both in the 'middle of nowhere' and exhibited favourable infrastructural connectivity and climatic conditions, especially during the winter months.

Based on an extension of this set of urban protocols, The Villages developed into a considerably larger masterplanned retirement community consisting mostly of detached 'single-family' houses, positioned on sculpted manmade landscapes of lawns and lakes. Each of the more than 50 'villages' is bordered by golf courses, lakes, pools and recreational centres, with a single gated entry and guardhouse.[5] Three 'downtowns' function as entertainment and retail centres, while additional retail and healthcare complexes resembling strip malls are located at points of contact between The Villages and the surrounding region.

Small-Town Metropolitanism: Scaling Up

According to a real-estate industry commentator, The Villages represents 'a retirement community on steroids'.[6] While it has not sought the status of incorporated city, as the largest single-site real-estate development in the US it has become large enough to qualify as a city in its own right, functioning as an important node within the regional network of towns and cities of central Florida.[7] It would, for example, constitute the state of Florida's sixteenth largest city, placing it above well-known cities such as Boca Raton or Daytona Beach. The community has reached a size capable of supporting its own substantial media business, called The Villages Media Group, owned by the developer.[8] Media holdings include three Villages-specific television stations, the *Villages Magazine*, a radio station and a newspaper, the *Villages Daily Sun*.[9]

Just as the sheer scale of The Villages is unprecedented, so too is its demographic singularity. Those aged between 60 and 85 years constitute 85.7 per cent of the population, 98.3 per cent are of white European ethnic descent, and 80.1 per cent of households are married couples.[10] Paradoxically, this leads to a simulated form of expanded urban scale as a result of the spatial concentration of such a homogeneous demographic group. While the demographic segment consisting of 'middle-class' retirees between 55 and 75 years of age constitutes the vast majority of the population at The Villages, in a conventional mixed urban setting that demographic segment would constitute only between 5 and 10 per cent of the total population. To locate the corresponding size of demographic segment of young-old, one would therefore have to identify a city between 10 and 20 times larger than The Villages: San Diego or Houston for example.[11]

Designed by Gary Mark, one of the original creators of Orlando's Universal Studios theme park, the three town squares of The Villages, including Lake Sumter Landing Market Square, shown here, re-enact the atmosphere of the small town of the youth of the current generation of residents.

Urban scale comparison. The Villages has achieved a new scale of age-segregated city.

The implications of this are evident in the staging of entertainment and cultural activities, and the deployment of local media – all focused on the demographic segment of the young-old. The organisers of events at The Villages are able to attract renowned musicians of the past, such as Lee Greenwood, to perform to large audiences that would typically be supported only by cities with larger populations. The Villages, therefore, often appears as an incongruous entry on the list of touring cities of such entertainers.

The clustering of this homogeneous demographic segment on such a large scale represents a further (and somewhat problematic) stage in the efficiency and rationalisation of the marketing and delivery of lifestyle products. It produces a socioeconomic and cultural centre of gravity in the region – a metropolitan condition for a particularly focused demographic entity. Ethical questions are raised over the 'benefits' of large mono-demographic enclaves such as local political evasion of tax burdens for public amenities including schools, that address other social or age groups.

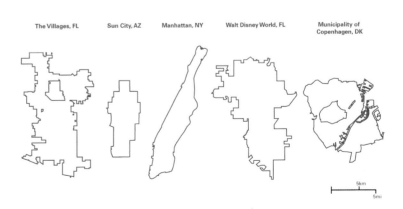

The Villages, FL   Sun City, AZ   Manhattan, NY   Walt Disney World, FL   Municipality of Copenhagen, DK

5km
5mi

Small-Town Metropolitanism: Scaling Down

Just as the demographic homogeneity of The Villages produces a scaling-up effect, this phenomenon is consciously countered by an opposing tendency: a scaling-down effect that involves the socio-spatial construction of a small town or village environment aligned to The Villages' slogan 'Florida's Friendliest Hometown'. The phrase is ubiquitous within the community, appearing on signs, banners, in print, on radio and television media, and in brochures advertising the lifestyle focus on small-town events such as parades, fairs and contests. Gary Morse, president and CEO of The Villages until his death in 2014, described the majority of residents as 'small town people' who 'would not want to retire to a big city', a sentiment reinforced in promotional videos that repeatedly refer to the development's 'friendly neighbours' and 'small-town charm'.[12]

The subdivision of the territory into smaller-sized neighbourhoods or 'villages' is the first component of the scaling-down strategy, breaking down the massive size of The Villages. Each individual village – with its own name, identity and amenities – forms the base unit within the development and the unit of securitisation and access. Rather than having a single large urban centre or downtown to service all inhabitants, The Villages' developer decided to build three 'small towns just like the small town we grew up in. There was another small town up the road a few miles in each direction.'[13] These form the core of social life, functioning as the second component of the scaling-down strategy.

The atmosphere of the small town is constructed through the themed design of the 'historic' town squares of the youth of the current cohort of residents, and was created by Gary Mark, one of the original designers of Orlando's Universal Studios theme park. The atmosphere of the countryside is deliberately evoked by a range of elements including wooden ranch-style fencing throughout the community, and a range of themed street furniture. Acknowledging his own background, having grown up in a small town and not wanting to retire to a large city, Morse recalled the scale of

Opening ceremony of the 2005 Florida Senior Olympics in Lake Sumter Landing Market Square. The community often hosts events of regional importance that belie its demographic scale. Its homogeneous population underwrites particular social distortions, for example a culture of youthfulness without youth.

The countryside as tabula rasa. Features of the existing landscape are literally scraped away to create a new canvas for the development protocols of the 'active adult' community.

the settlement as more familiar to the collective housing of his generation. This affinity to the small town is reinforced by urban versus suburban rural population statistics at particular moments of his generation: in 1940, for example, 52 per cent of the population of the US was living in non-metropolitan areas (cities or districts with less than 100,000 inhabitants), but by 2000 that figure had diminished to 20 per cent.[14]

The suggestion of the small town's intrinsic appropriateness for retirement in comparison to the city may also be linked to the dominant alienation and fear of urban living by the white middle class from the postwar period onwards, together with the challenges ascribed to the sprawl of suburbia and exurbia from the 1980s to the 2000s. In these terms, affinities to the rhetoric of the New Urbanists can be identified, particularly the intention of Andrés Duany' and Elizabeth Plater-Zyberk to realise 'The Second Coming of the American Small Town'[15] as an antidote to the shortcomings of urban sprawl.

The New Urbanist project to reinstate a scale and form of community-based living rooted in a cultural vernacular overlaps with the intention of The Villages to re-create an idealised size and atmosphere of urban ensembles based in part on a constructed collective nostalgia for a small hometown – when things were 'simpler', when one could walk everywhere, and when everyone knew everyone else's name. This is further manifested in social interactions – as a form of pseudo-familiarity in which it is customary for strangers to greet other strangers as friends or acquaintances as if in a small town. While not necessarily involving extended communications, an extraordinary 'friendliness' exists – particularly evident in the 'town squares' – through greetings such as 'Hi ya buddy', 'Mornin'', 'How ya doin', and so forth. This tendency may be understood as a product of the theming and branding techniques in play,

supported by the local media construct of 'Florida's Friendliest Hometown' as a form of social behaviour propaganda. It is also supported by the homogeneity of residents providing an extremely limited presence of an identifiable, feared 'other' (whether defined economically, ethnically, racially or in terms of age).

As an extension of the scalar manipulations described here, what emerges is an interesting by-product of the scale of the community, its spatial isolation in the 'middle of nowhere' and its status as a mono-demographic enclave. In particular, a lack of a surrounding younger population base large enough to fill the necessary service jobs in the community. Within an environment constitutionally based on leisure – and 'the vacation that never ends' – it is ironic that so many residents engage in second 'careers' after retirement, whether on a part-time or full-time basis, for fun or out of economic necessity. For example, a retired police officer and his wife (a retired schoolteacher) run an electronic organ store in The Villages as well as offering lessons to interested residents.

Diagram of small-town metropolitanism at The Villages. Articulating the scalar elastics of The Villages in graphic form, the diagram maps a third position between that of the conventional village and the city, in which stimulation becomes possible (without alienation) and familiarity (without boredom).

Scalar Elastics

It is according to these paired tendencies that The Villages produces an elastic form of urban scaling. While scaling-up tendencies support the elimination of the programmatic 'boredom' of small-town or rural life enabled by a demographically concentrated form of urban 'stimulation', scaling-down effects attempt to diminish the social 'alienation' of the large city or exurbia through the simulation of the aesthetic and behavioural 'familiarity' of the small town in the countryside. This short-circuits Georg Simmel's classical construction of the psychological condition of the metropolitan dweller – typified by the paired characteristics of stimulation and alienation – in contrast to the small town, village or countryside coupling of familiarity and boredom.[16] Just as the Garden City of Ebenezer Howard intended to merge the positive characteristics of the city with those of the countryside – without the ill effects of either – The Villages attempts to perform its own specific kind of Howardian pact – albeit one made at considerable environmental and societal cost. A compact designed to send residents back to a constructed, idealised mental space of a less urban and more rural past – the space of their own youth where stimulation might be possible without alienation, and familiarity without boredom. ⏎

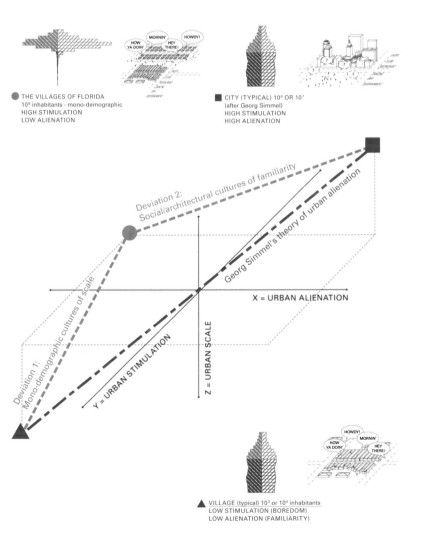

THE VILLAGES OF FLORIDA
10^5 inhabitants · mono-demographic
HIGH STIMULATION
LOW ALIENATION

CITY (TYPICAL) 10^6 OR 10^7
(after Georg Simmel)
HIGH STIMULATION
HIGH ALIENATION

Deviation 2:
Social/architectural cultures of familiarity

Georg Simmel's theory of urban alienation

X = URBAN ALIENATION

Deviation 1:
Mono-demographic cultures of scale

Y = URBAN STIMULATION

Z = URBAN SCALE

VILLAGE (typical) 10^3 or 10^4 inhabitants
LOW STIMULATION (BOREDOM)
LOW ALIENATION (FAMILIARITY)

Notes

1. Jacob Pramuk, 'The Villages, FL – America's Fastest-Growing Metro Area', CNBC, 26 March 2015: www.cnbc.com/2015/03/26/the-villages-fl-americas-fastest-growing-metro-area.html.
2. H Gary Morse, 'Yesterday, Today and Tomorrow!', *The Villages Daily Sun*, 2007, p 1.
3. *Ibid*.
4. Andrew Blechman, *Leisureville: Adventures in America's Retirement Utopias*, Atlantic Monthly Press (New York), 2008, p. 43.
5. H Gary Morse, *op cit*. As of 2015 most of the planned 91 recreational centres, 69 pools and 47 golf courses were completed.
6. Blechman, *op cit*, p. 39.
7. The Villages Commercial Property and Sales Leasing, 'The Villages Market': www.thevillagescommercialproperty.com/the-villages-market.asp.
8. US Census Bureau, American FactFinder, 'Annual Estimates of the Resident Population for Incorporated Places of 50,000 or More, Ranked by July 1, 2014', 21 February 2016: http://factfinder.census.gov/faces/tableservices/jsf/pages/productview.xhtml?src=bkmk.
9. The Villages Commercial Property and Sales Leasing, *op cit*. According to the website, *The Villages Daily Sun* was 'ranked #1 among US newspapers in circulation growth in 2006', and boasted an average paid daily circulation of 35,808.
10. US Census Bureau, American FactFinder, 'ACS Demographic and Housing Estimates: 2008–2012 American Community Survey 5-Year Estimates': http://factfinder2.census.gov/faces/tableservices/jsf/pages/productview.xhtml?pid=ACS_12_5YR_DP05.
11. *Ibid*.
12. H Gary Morse, *op cit*, p 1.
13. *Ibid*.
14. Frank Hobbs and Nicole Stoops, 'Demographic Trends in the 20th Century: Census 2000 Special Reports', US Census Bureau, November 2002, pp 32–3: www.census.gov/prod/2002pubs/censr-4.pdf.
15. Andrés Duany and Elizabeth Plater-Zyberk, 'The Second Coming of the American Small Town', *Wilson Quarterly*, Winter 1992, pp 19–50.
16. Georg Simmel, 'The Metropolis and Mental Life' [1903], in Gary Bridge and Sophie Watson, *The Blackwell City Reader*, Blackwell (Oxford and Malden, MA), 2002, pp 11–19.

New Territories

Division: Yuen Long,
New Territories,
Hong Kong,
2014

Deconstructing and Constructing Countryside

–

The Great Divide of Rural and Urban in Hong Kong

When mass immigration led to a sixfold population increase in the first two postwar decades, the Hong Kong government's response was to build nine new towns, designate 40 per cent of the land as country parks for urban dwellers' benefit, and allocate buildable plots as compensation to displaced villagers. Guest-Editor **Christiane Lange** examines how these well-meaning efforts broke the cultural and social ties between people and the land that are essential to sustaining a productive rural landscape: a cautionary tale for designers and planners involved in developing the countryside.

The New Territories in Hong Kong (comprising the rural area between urban Kowloon and mainland China, and making up more than 86 per cent of Hong Kong's total area) has transformed from a purposeful landscape serving a working rural community to a collage of reconstructed and deconstructed countryside merged with the detritus of urban development and crumbled rural institutions. The Hong Kong colonial government's impetus to develop infrastructure in rural areas changed gear in the 1960s, shifting to address the pressures of an increased population and rampant urbanisation in the territory at that time. Policy interventions were put in place to tightly moderate the urban footprint and contain urban expansion within a series of new towns. Meanwhile, a network of country parks constructed an idea and an image of the countryside to serve the urban core of Hong Kong rather than a rural population.

Policy interventions in the countryside were consequently intentionally minimal, unwittingly leaving indigenous villages to implode in the wake of the forces of urbanisation around them. As an unregulated urbanisation spilt over into these rural areas and gathered increasing momentum, it broke down the ties and institutional structures that had governed ideas of responsibility and ownership within the landscape. The experience of the New Territories in Hong Kong thus raises questions of global relevance about how best to design and develop a rural landscape in the wake of increasing urbanisation.

Old Territory (On the Perception of Countryside)

Inhabited by indigenous clans since early AD 900, the New Territories retained its own land rights and worked to its own laws. It was picturesque: paddy fields and vernacular Chinese walled-village clusters were framed by sea and mountains in the lowlands while the valleys of the New Territories lay spread about them. For the first half of the 20th century and earlier, the scenery would have been reminiscent of that in ancient ink drawings of agrarian Chinese societies that lived in accordance with ideas of Feng Shui – the philosophical system of harmonising everyone with their surrounding environment.

Approximately 80,000 long-settled villagers, members of close-knit clans, lived in over 700 villages in this region. Just before taking over the area that would soon be called the New Territories, Governor Blake of the British Colony of Hong Kong promised villagers in a proclamation dated 7 April 1899 that their commercial and landed interests would 'be safeguarded, and [their] usages and good customs ... not in any way be interfered with'. 'Within the leased area,' he stated, 'all fields, land, houses, graves, local customs and usages will remain unchanged, only if land is required for public offices, fortifications, or the like official purposes, it shall be bought at a fair price.'[1] This was soon to become a complicated proposition.

Division: Yuen Long, New Territories, Hong Kong, 2014

Top-down management of the rural and its separation into new towns, country parks and village land has amplified the urban–rural divide.

New Territories (On the Force of Urbanisation)

The New Territories were leased to the British Crown Colony of Hong Kong for 99 years from Qing China, under the 1898 Peking Convention. The policies of the colonial government in the mid-20th century focused on developing the rural sector and services for the agrarian sector. With the establishment of the Agricultural, Forestry and Fisheries Department in 1946, the following years saw the introduction of better sanitation and water supply, markets, communication networks, postal and bank services and public primary schools – all with the aim of incrementally improving the livelihoods of the rural community.[2] However, these policies shifted as the global forces of industrialisation and capitalism began to gain momentum and the development of the export-led manufacturing industry in Hong Kong began to boom in the 1950s. Hong Kong became one of the most important trading points between East and West. Farming became less profitable than other lines of work, and villagers of the New Territories began turning away from their land and focusing instead on the opportunities the new economy afforded them.

```
Abandonment: Yuen Long,
New Territories,
Hong Kong,
2015
```

below left and right: Urban-sector encroachment has led to the deconstruction of the rural: literally in terms of built heritage, and figuratively in terms of socioeconomic structures.

The Old Territory and The New Territory (On the Division of Rural and Urban)

Migrants from mainland China, meanwhile, escaping the communist government and the Great Leap Forward (1958–61), flooded into what would become the densest urban agglomeration on a 'bare rock'[3] – Hong Kong Island and the Kowloon Peninsula. In just 20 years, the population grew by over 600 per cent. By the 1960s this growth in population and the subsequent severe land shortages had stretched the 'city' and the available housing in Hong Kong to its limits. In the Kowloon Peninsula, 1.5 million people were living on roughly 3,000 hectares (7,400 acres).

In response to the increasing urban population and their requirements for housing and recreational areas, the colonial government shifted from incremental rural development to addressing the needs of the urban sector. A two-pronged approach was developed: the Public Housing Programme Scheme, realised through the building of new towns within the New Territories, and the Country Park Scheme that sought to preserve the natural environment of the countryside to serve urban recreational needs. This policy decision was taken after 1965 when Lee Talbot of the International Commission on National Parks was consulted to outline areas for nature conservation and recreation that would protect Hong Kong's biotic environment.

The Talbot report recommended the creation of a system of rural parks, recreation areas and reserves in the territory: 'In view of the rapidly increasing pressures on the land expanding and often unplanned use made of present open space … time is critical. If the establishment of a park system is delayed long, the open spaces where it can be established almost certainly will no longer exist.'[4] Talbot pointed out that 'the more urbanized and industrialized a country becomes, the greater the need of its inhabitants to find open space for recreation, away from the high pressure, artificial world they have created … People needed recreation areas and wild open spaces to rest and contemplate, where they could hike, camp, climb, bird-watch or just enjoy nature'.[5] Sir Murray MacLehose, appointed Governor of Hong Kong in 1971 and an outdoors enthusiast, supported the Talbot report, and the Country Parks Ordinance of 1976 established 21 country parks in the territory covering 40,000 hectares (98,840 acres), or 40 per cent of Hong Kong's total area, which remains designated in this way today.

The Public Housing Programme Scheme, meanwhile, developed nine 'new towns' in the New Territories along the lines of the public housing model in modern Britain. Based on high-rise and high density, the satellite towns occupy 8,800 hectares (21,745 acres), of which 3,000 hectares (7,410 acres) are reclaimed from the sea. They house 3.4 million people – half of Hong Kong's population today. Working towards Modernist ideals, the new towns superimposed top-down planning on what were hitherto rural areas. Ideas of the countryside began to shift from images of the rural ink-drawing landscape to those of a recreational site or nature sanctuary for the urban dweller. But realising this pre-constructed image of the countryside came at the cost of loosening the ties of the indigenous village community to their land.

Villagers affected by the development of the new towns or country parks were allocated land as compensation. One aspect of this was the colonial government's introduction in 1972 of the Small House Policy, under which each male villager over 18 years of age gained the right and a concessionary grant, upon marriage, to build a three-storey, 700 square metre (7,535 square foot) concrete house. This birthright of the *ding* (male), or son of the family was aimed at allowing village areas to develop in accordance with their independent needs. With the lack of a coherent strategy to develop or support rural livelihoods and infrastructure, the Small House Policy became leverage for those with rural land to enter the urban sector. However, this encroachment of the urban into the rural led to a further deconstruction of the rural: literally in terms of built heritage, and figuratively in terms of socioeconomic structures. Up until today there has been little meaningful involvement in rural development from the Hong Kong (SAR) Government, urban planners, architects or conservators.

Segregation: Yuen Long,
New Territories,
Hong Kong,
2014

both images: Dividing the rural and urban has segregated the indigenous population, marginalising their culture and thus their socio-cultural ties to the land.

Working towards Modernist ideals, the new towns superimposed top-down planning on what were hitherto rural areas.

The hole in policy has played itself out to foster a physical Deconstructivist collage of a countryside that is evident when walking through the New Territories today: a colonial church from 1928 now used as a trash collection point; an ancient Chinese study hall from the late 18th century that has been turned into a car park; a village watch tower from the early 20th century left to decay; farmland taken over by the harbour for container storage, or in some cases by the construction industry as an illegal dump site. Themed leisure environments with collapsed piles of 200-year-old yellow loam bricks lie next to developers' middle-class enclaves echoing designs of American suburbia, while high-tech Mass Transit Railway (MTR) high-lines and giant, monotonous new towns, built in the spirit of the Modernist ideals, have cast out walled, dark-brick village settlements. Some of these settlements are still intact, some have grown and spilled out of their walled forts, while others have been abandoned and left to decay. Today it is only the country parks hovering over the new and old territory, guided by a preconceived idea of the countryside, that offer resistance to the high pressure of urban development with their status as a protected network of urban wilderness.

New Territories (On the Design of the Countryside)

Landscape has ethical, environmental and aesthetic dimensions and the countryside is considered the scenery that embeds those concepts. Traditionally, it has been governed in the best interests of the community indigenous to the land, by individual landowners, families and villages that took responsibility over the formulation of their landscape. While the relationship of villagers to their customs, land and thus their culture has been adversely affected in Hong Kong, ideas of the countryside have been constructed for the urban dweller. The environmental recreational opportunities afforded to them by restricted country parks coupled with the idea of high-density living in the countryside as an antidote or respite to urban living have forged a great divide between the urban and rural, and between people and land.

This radical divide of rural and urban, featuring a one-sided approach for the rural to fulfil the needs of the urban, has altered social and cultural ties to the land, which has in turn been neglected, leading to the deconstruction of the landscape. To develop and design the countryside, planners and architects need to reformulate these ties and responsibilities back into the landscapes by carefully depicting and drawing from cultural references, and by the adequate and informed governance of spatial frameworks that not only bridge the divide between urban and rural, but also allow people to once again reference their lives to the land. ∆

Notes

1. Hong Kong Government, Government Notification No 201, Appendix IV, 'English version of Chinese Proclamation' by Sir Henry Arthur Blake GCMG, British colonial administrator and Governor-General of Hong Kong from 1898 to 1903, p xx, Supplement to *Government Gazette*, 1900: http://sunzi.lib.hku.hk/hkgro/view/g1900/507133.pdf
2. See James Hayes, 'The Great Difference, The Great Rift and the Great Need: The New Territories and its People, Past and Present', *Asia Pacific Journal of Public Administration*, 30 (2), December 2008, pp 139–64.
3. Hong Kong is often referred to as a 'bare rock'.
4. See Lee Merriam Talbot and Martha H Talbot, *Conservation of the Hong Kong Countryside: Summary Report and Recommendation*, S. Young, Government Printer (Hong Kong), 1965, p 23.
5. *Ibid*, p 16.

Deconstruction: Yuen Long, New Territories, Hong Kong, 2014

above and right: The laissez-faire attitude and involvement of both the colonial and Hong Kong (SAR) governments has resulted in today's deconstructed countryside.

Charlotte Malterre-Barthes

The Toshka Project

Mubarak Pumping Station,
Lake Nasser,
2005

The largest pumping station ever
built was inaugurated by the then-
President of Egypt Hosni Mubarak
and named after him.

Colossal Water Infrastructures, Biopolitics and Territory in Egypt

Incorporating the world's largest ever pumping station, the Toshka Project sets out to make a vast area of Egypt's Western Desert suitable for agriculture, industry and habitation, both assisting national food security and relieving pressure

Here, the political, social, national, and military battles of the Egyptian people materialize as the bulk of the great rock which blocked the old Nile waterway, to accumulate its waters into the biggest lake ever made by man, as a permanent source of prosperity.

—

Gamal Abdel Nasser,
14 May 1964.[1]

In a dark suit, wearing aviator-style glasses, President Hosni Mubarak is standing firmly, arm on the railing, overlooking blue waters. The pumping station that carries his name is towering in the background. This scene occurred in 2005, during one of many visits of the then-President of Egypt to the Toshka Project, which includes the largest pumping station ever built, a 310-kilometre (193-mile) long water channel and a target of a million hectares (2.5 million acres) of irrigated fields for crops and fruits. This is all part of a 'New Nile Valley' vision that includes three schemes – Toshka, Oweinat and the New Valley oases – aimed at converting part of the Western Desert into an agricultural and industrial area.

President Mubarak inspected various stages of the construction site at the Toshka Depression, in the desert region west of Lake Nasser. His visits, spanning from the late 1990s to the mid-2000s, attest to the political relevance of water infrastructures for Egyptian governing powers, and the desire of the regime to exhibit confidence in a scheme that claimed to solve water supply, food security and overpopulation issues through its gigantic enterprise. They also confirm that Toshka is a presidential project, positioning its champion in the long lineage of Egyptian rulers who have embarked on large-scale schemes.

There is, in Egypt, a legacy of monumental water projects presented as national technological achievements, such as the High Aswan Dam. Scholars argue that these projects have served as governmental instruments of political hegemony and social control, fostering national pride and diverting attention from other issues.[2] Toshka is one of the most recent projects in a long list of irrigation and hydraulic infrastructures partially inspired by colonial technocracy and associated with agricultural prosperity (for example, the Delta Barrages, Assiut Barrage, Low Aswan Dam, Century Storage Scheme, Western Oasis Project and High

on cities to accommodate a growing population. Architect and urban designer **Charlotte Malterre-Barthes** evaluates the project and sets it in the context of a long line of ambitious territorial transformation and irrigation schemes centred around the Nile.

Aswan Dam). In the historical nation-building discourse of Egyptian *Grands Plans*, it appears to be another political and territorial act, involving foreign and national actors and financial capitals, implemented in the name of food security. It materialises as a spatially grounded biopolitical instrument with social, economic and political factors affecting the built environment and shaping territory.

Because, as Michel Foucault argued, biopolitics originated when politics ceased to be seen as an extension of war and instead as a tool to control, regulate and manage the lives of populations in the service of the state, and is now more concerned with the administration of life itself, food security is a regulatory instrument to politically control and manage life in a way similar to the control exerted over food production and supply.[3] Toshka and its preceding modern water infrastructures are thus the physical manifestations of this phenomenon; namely how, under global pressure, the pursuit of national food self-sufficiency is used to justify large-scale territorial transformations towards chimerical agricultural opulence. Echoing the legacy of the High Aswan Dam, Toshka exemplifies how colossal hydro-infrastructures inserted in rural areas redefine and redesign territory – the massive diversion of water flows, the magnitude of topographical modifications, the construction of large-scale structures, buildings or new transportation networks, the envisioned relocation of 20 per cent of the population (16 million people) – with tremendous political, climatic and topographical consequences.

There is no need to resort to biblical narratives of plagues and famines to recognise that, for Egypt, the fertilising sediments carried by its river were imperative to ensure local food production. Thus the fine balance between appropriate irrigation and floods was a matter of life and death. In this context, for hundreds of years Egypt has sought to secure the flow of water down the Nile to ensure

Infrastructural chronicle of the Nile in Egyptian territory, 1862–2005

This modern infrastructural chronicle of the river displays how successive powers have attempted, exponentially so, to control the Nile to achieve their declared goals of food security, agricultural innovation and industrialisation, and their vested political ambitions. Egypt's rulers have thus contributed to the creation of a body of controlling devices and regulatory instruments concerned with the administration of the population through the management of water and food production.

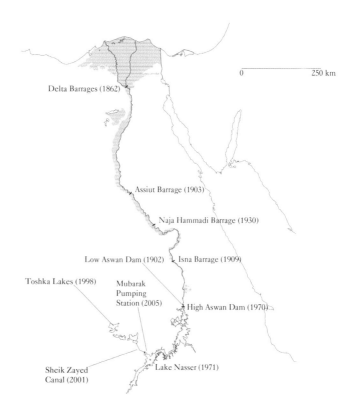

Delta Barrages (1862)

0 250 km

Assiut Barrage (1903)

Naja Hammadi Barrage (1930)

Low Aswan Dam (1902)   Isna Barrage (1909)

Toshka Lakes (1998)   Mubarak Pumping Station (2005)

High Aswan Dam (1970)

Sheik Zayed Canal (2001)   Lake Nasser (1971)

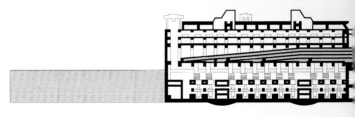

Mougel Bey, Delta Barrages,
Rosetta and Damietta
branches of the Nile,
Egypt, 1862

The Delta Barrages, ordered by Khedive
Muhammad Ali Pasha, were the first
modern infrastructural works on the
Egyptian Nile. Planned by French engineers
and located at the Nile division between the
Rosetta and Damietta branches, they were
completed in 1862, but never succeeded
in resisting Nile flooding despite several
reparation works. They are currently used
as bridges.

Intake canal   Pumping station

its food supply – in the process straining diplomatic relations
with neighbouring countries Sudan and Ethiopia. In fact, the
political history of the Egyptian nation-state is indissociable
from that of the river and its control, with both national
and colonial rulers relying on the construction of modern
infrastructures to regulate water levels and ensure food
security, resulting in territorial transformations as a physical
expression of biopolitics.

Egypt's history of hydraulic management and artificial
irrigation spans centuries, with the Nile a managed river
since Pharaonic times, flooding annually with a predictable
regularity. The floodwaters were channelled into reservoirs
or irrigation waterways along *feddans*,[4] pumped and
distributed according to a complex hierarchy, and eventually
released to the river in an intricate mechanism called basin
irrigation. Despite claims that colonial Britain brought
progress to 19th-century Egypt in the form of engineering,
it was the Khedive Muhammad Ali Pasha, Ottoman viceroy
of Egypt, who first ordered that infrastructural measures be
taken to harness the Nile waters in the modern era, partially
inspired by the studies of French scientists who accompanied
Napoleon's army.[5] Integrated within Ali's political project,
the modernisation of the irrigation system was to establish
the nation's strength and independence. Under his rule,
Egyptian agriculture, which had relied on yearly floodwaters
to produce only one major crop a year, shifted from basin
irrigation to a perennial irrigation system, expanding a
network of deep canals in the Delta.[6] Rapidly, a modern
perennial irrigation system was implemented, partly to
improve the cultivation of cotton, with floodwaters stored
in reservoirs to be used throughout the year, and barrages
damming the Nile to raise its water level.[7]

The first modern infrastructural works on the Egyptian
Nile that aimed to increase agricultural production grown
out of national demand were the Delta Barrages, planned by

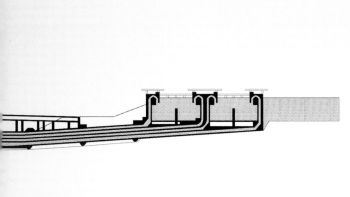

The first modern infrastructural works on the Egyptian Nile that aimed to increase agricultural production grown out of national demand were the Delta Barrages, planned by French engineers and completed in 1862.

Discharge ducts — — — — — Discharge basins — — —

0 5 15 30 m

Mubarak Pumping Station, Toshka Project, Lake Nasser, Egypt, 2005

Inaugurated in 2005, the Mubarak Pumping Station supplies the Sheik Zayed Canal with Lake Nasser water to irrigate the sands of the Western Desert and is the centrepiece of the Toshka Project. Built by a consortium of international and local companies, the station is surrounded by water in a 50-metre (164-foot) deep intake channel with 24 vertical pumps with an intake capacity of 400 cubic metres (14,125 cubic feet) a second.

French engineers and located at the Nile division between the Rosetta and Damietta branches, and completed in 1862. It quickly surfaced, however, that the Delta Barrages had structural flaws and could not resist Nile floods. Two decades later, as financial collapse loomed, Egypt became a British protectorate. Colonial forces came to Egypt with technocratic beliefs 'in the powers of technology in the form of irrigation infrastructures', disdainful towards Muhammad Ali's efforts to control floods, guarantee food security and promote cotton production.[8] While the Delta Barrages marked the start of irrigation works of the 19th century, it was their failure in restraining the floods that prompted the construction of the Low Aswan Dam. The primary motivation of the British for erecting another dam was to retain water year-round, as the colonial administration was shifting from a culture of sustenance food crops to an export-oriented cotton economy, concealed in a discourse of modernisation and a Western conception that the Nile waters were previously underutilised. Based on such assumptions, and with the underlying aim of serving foreign interests and fueling European banks with repayments of debt generated by building the Suez Canal, further hydraulic infrastructures began to be established along the Nile.

Under British supervision, the Low Aswan Dam was completed in 1902.[9] However, it too proved insufficient and had to be raised several times. When it threatened to overflow for a third time in 1946, the decision was made to build a second dam a few miles upstream – a decision that was confirmed after the overthrowing of the monarch by Gamal Abdel Nasser's Free Officers. Based on a Modernist rationale, the first Aswan Dam paved the way for the largest hydro-power infrastructure based on foreign expertise in Egypt: the High Aswan Dam. Motivations for its construction spanned from energy production to Cold War political arrangements, yet for Nasser the primary objective

Sheik Zayed Canal,
Toshka,
Egypt

Fed by Lake Nasser water
via the Mubarak Pumping
Station, the Sheik Zayed
Canal, though only partially
completed, sustains some
agricultural activities
in constricted fields on
previously desert land.

The Sheik Zayed Canal, created
8 kilometres (5 miles) north of
the Toshka Spillway and supplied
with Lake Nasser water by the
Mubarak Pumping Station to
irrigate the sands of the Western
Desert, marked the first phase
of the Toshka Project.

was to feed the Egyptian population by improving irrigation
and enabling large desert reclamation schemes for agriculture.
It is no surprise, therefore, that it was from this massive dam
(5 kilometres/3 miles long and 100 metres/328 feet high) and
the Lake Nasser reservoir's 163,000 cubic kilometers (almost
40,000 cubic miles) that the Toshka Project originated.

In 1966, to prevent any downstream or backflow
flooding, an overflow canal named the Toshka Spillway
was excavated on the western shore of Lake Nasser into
the Toshka Depression. While it remained unused, Egyptian
engineers saw in the spillway the potential to turn the Toshka
Depression into lakes and reclaim desert land[10] – an idea that
was revived when, in 1996, the Nile waters overflowed into
the canal.[11] A new waterway, the Sheik Zayed Canal, created
8 kilometres (5 miles) north of the Toshka Spillway and
supplied with Lake Nasser water by the Mubarak Pumping
Station to irrigate the sands of the Western Desert, marked
the first phase of the Toshka Project.

Ultimately, the aim of the project is to irrigate 540,000
feddans (approximately 226,800 hectares/560,520 acres) and
for it to become home to 20 per cent of Egyptians to alleviate
pressure on the country's crowded cities. A public project of
unprecedented scale and a slow pace of construction, it relies
on development aid from several countries and organisations
as well as on private investors. Presented as Mubarak's solution
for Egypt's urban density, food insecurity and unemployment
in one massive project involving complex arrangements of
foreign investments and expertise, experts claim the project
has failed to deliver. High saline levels mean that fresh water is
less than expected, employment opportunities are low, housing
and infrastructure have yet to materialise and, ultimately, food
production at Toshka is concentrated on profitable export
crops for foreign companies rather than on food for domestic
consumption, breaking the initial promise of local agricultural
production for food security.[12]

Irrigated grain
fields, Toshka,
Egypt,
2012

The Kingdom Agricultural
Development Company
(KADCO) is a private
agribusiness owned by
Prince Walid Bin Talal from
Saudi Arabia that invested in
the Toshka Project. The firm
produces cash crops for
exports.

Shaping Egypt's agricultural system has meant rearranging its territory and population through the ordering and managing of earth and water. In this sense, the evolution of modern biopolitics and the discourse on food security finds no better terrain. The experts' constructed image of Egypt as a country on the brink of starvation with scarce agrarian land and explosive demographics, as denounced by Timothy Mitchell in *Rule of Experts*, epitomises how Egyptian political forces have engaged in undertaking gigantic projects against the backdrop of its long historical legacy of water infrastructures.[13] Under the cover of achieving food security, modern gigantic projects such as Toshka have been an essential element of Egyptian politics. The control over water, land, topography, population, and agricultural and food production revealed by the infrastructural chronicle of the river is a recurrent story of power struggles over territory, people and resources. Egypt is thus a paradigmatic case where contemporary biopolitics are deployed and where the ensuing spatial consequences on rural territories, such as at Toshka, are acutely visible. ⚭

Under the cover of achieving food security, modern gigantic projects such as Toshka have been an essential element of Egyptian politics.

Notes
1. Extract from Gamal Abdel Nasser's speech on the occasion of the diversion of the Nile River, 14 May 1964. See www.nasser.org/Speeches/browser. aspx?SID=1084&lang=en.
2. Jeroen Warner, 'The Toshka Mirage in the Egyptian Desert: River Diversion as Political Diversion', *Environmental Science & Policy*, 30, 2013, pp 102–12.
3. See Michel Foucault, *Society Must Be Defended: Lectures at the Collège De France*, 1975–1976, eds Michel Senellart, François Ewald and Alessandro Fontana, Picador (New York), 2003.
4. The *feddan* is a unit of area used in Egypt, Sudan and Syria. 1 feddan = 24 kirat = 60 x 70 metres = 4,200 square metres = 0.42 hectares = 1.038 acres.
5. Timothy Mitchell, *Rule of Experts: Egypt, Techno-Politics, Modernity*, University of California Press (Berkeley, CA), 2002, p 35.
6. Bibliothéque municipale de Marseille, *Pascal Coste, Toutes Les Egypte*, Parenthèses (Marseille), 1998, p 40.
7. AB Zahlan and Rosemarie Said Zahlan, 'Established Patterns of Technology Acquisition in the Arab World', *Technology Transfer and Change in the Arab World: The Proceedings of a Seminar of the United Nations Economic Commission for Western Asia*, United Nations and Pergamon Press (Oxford and New York), 1978, pp 1–128.
8. Diana K Davis, Edmund Burke and Timothy Mitchell, *Environmental Imaginaries of the Middle East and North Africa*, Ohio University Press (Athens, OH), 2011, p 6.
9. Travis Cook, 'Engineering Modernity: The Aswan Low Dam and Modernizing the Nile', Department of History capstone paper, Western Oregon University (Monmouth, OR), 2013.
10. MM Sayed and MM Kamal, 'Flood Evaluation and Management after the High Dam Reservoir', *Proceedings of the International Symposium on Dams in the Societies of the 21st Century*, ICOLD, Taylor & Francis (London), 2006, pp 47–52.
11. Robert O Collins, 'Negotiations and Exploitation of the Nile Waters at the End of the Millennium', *Water International*, 31, 1, 2006, pp 116–26.
12. Bradley Hope, 'Egypt's New Nile Valley: Grand Plan Gone Bad', *The National*, 22 April 2012: www.thenational. ae/news/world/middle-east/egypts-new-nile-valley-grand-plan-gone-bad.
13. See Mitchell, *op cit*, p 209.

Stephan Petermann

Denniston International Architects,
The Chedi Andermatt,
Andermatt,
Switzerland,
2013

Smack planning Andermatt: 'When we started developing we had a main
concern: there is an existing village. It has been here for hundreds
of years and we must respect that. It is really for this reason we put our
largest hotels smack in the centre of the village.' Quote from Samih Sawari
in 'The Making of Andermatt', 2012: https://youtu.be/bvgF3ejMd6l.

Best of Both Worlds

Lamenting Our Path to the Future

SkiArena Andermatt-Sedrun

Andermatt Village Centre

The Chedi Andermatt

Golf Clubhouse

Train Station

Golf Course

Gotthard Residences
4-Star Hotel

Apartment Houses
Chalets

After a period of decline, the Alpine valley of Andermatt in Switzerland is undergoing major development as a holiday resort by an Egyptian real-estate billionaire. A documentary film on the process, by a young Swiss filmmaker, highlights the ambivalent relationship between global corporatist efforts to 'rescue' struggling rural areas, and the local communities concerned. **Stephan Petermann**, who is researching the future of the countryside for architect Rem Koolhaas's think tank AMO, gives an account of it.

Andermatt masterplan

Three core components: the central Chedi resort with 50 hotel rooms and 119 residences for sale, the large urban addition outside of the village, and the 18-hole golf course. Extensive upgrading of the ski slopes is also currently underway.

'Do I dare
Disturb the universe?'

— TS Eliot, 'The Love Song of J Alfred Prufrock', 1917[1]

Thaw rises from the Andermatt Valley in the heart of Switzerland, a stone's throw away from the Gotthard Pass. A thriving holiday destination for the European elite prior to the Second World War, after the war it housed a large military base as part of the Swiss Alpine Fortress. As the base closed at the end of the Cold War, Andermatt lost its single source of income, devastating the local economy. It had missed the touristic development spree that had saved other sleepy Swiss communities and didn't know what to do. Until an Egyptian sun-ray hit the village. In 2008 a helicopter crosses the valley. On board, Egyptian billionaire real-estate tycoon Samih Sawiris. Herr Sawiris 'discovers' Andermatt and decides to 'buy' its valley and develop it.

Swansong

AMO learnt about the project in 2009, as part of its initial explorations of a new focus on the countryside. The current urban triumphalism – the perpetual flow of books and biennales that celebrate the cliché that more than half of mankind now lives in urban conditions – created the perfect alibi for the studio to look in the rear-view mirror at what is left behind: a radicalising political, social and economic landscape determined by neo-Cartesian tech-driven orthodoxies, contours of a market economy in its purest form. Amid numerous reports of Zeppelin hangers, former military strongholds, historical country estates and entire villages bought by celebrities and venture capitalists on their way to 'resortification', the Andermatt development showed a fragment of this new agency between decay and exotic-sounding futures. In 2015, Andermatt resurfaced in a documentary film by Leonidas Bieri, who systematically tracks the evolution of Sawiris's project, its events and the lives of related characters. Disturbingly like a Greek tragedy, the film leaves one wary about what is actually being documented and, more specifically, of its subtitle: 'Global Village'.

Line-Up

The premise: Sawiris's group Orascom Hotels and Development invests in a series of developments in and around the centre of Andermatt. The first is the Chedi, a five-star resort hotel opened in 2013, shaped as a group of connected supersized Swiss chalets, 'smacked' in the centre of the village.[2] The second phase is a large-scale masterplan development at the village perimeter with a mix of (holiday) housing and hotels. Third is the launch of a plan to enhance leisure quality by expanding skiing and golf facilities. A referendum was held in 2009: 90 per cent of the population affirmed the plans and all is currently under construction or has been finished.

A somewhat expected cast of characters appears in the documentary: a league of 'bad' project-developer blowhards ('Andermatt is now getting into the Champions League of tourism'); a devout hotel owner/manager (dubiously cited wanting to 'eliminate' anyone in the village not part of the high-income prospective clients); an executive architect thankful for employment taking orders from a multi-continental team from Kuala Lumpur (design architect), Melbourne (lighting designer), Hong Kong (kitchen designer) and Miami (tree specialist); a mountain-crystal-cutting elderly local ('They are ruining the village'); a 20-year-old staying in the village because of the improved prospects ('Andermatt was very lucky to land the deal'); and a choir of grunting middle-aged local men in pubs questioning the dubious tax breaks given to Sawiris ('Sawiris has been exempted from capital gains tax for 10 years!').

The movie itself is a habitual wrestling through muddy situations: the ease with which its architects created shiny PR material leaves the movie as a counter-mould reality check. Unexpected delays on the construction further accelerate its development speed. Ambitions are delicately lowered by the developer through press events. The psychology of the village takes a blow as villagers realise it is not the pot of gold they thought it to be. Most ironically, it is illustrated, literally, in mud: an enormous tree is transported to the village and placed in front of the hotel – an exact copy of the existing trees surrounding it, as proposed by the tree consultant from Miami. Restless men show up in the pub: despite their clear anger, it remains unclear what their dissatisfaction really entails. Is it simple envy of the flashy has-it-all guy? Self-pity? What is it they are offended by? And what does the Teflon-politician-like appearance of Sawiris reveal?

Leonidas Bieri,
Andermatt: Global Village,
DOCIME,
2015

Max Germann, architect in charge, explaining the Chedi Andermatt design to previous elderly inhabitants of the site: 'We are the executive architects. We didn't design this project. It was designed by a reputed hotel architect Denniston from Kuala Lumpur.'

Arrested Development

Andermatt's two most engaging protagonists are a banished farmer and the real-estate mogul. The farmer, probably in his late 30s, is a straightforward, hearty and somewhat foolish Don Quichotte-en-boîte. Bieri documents his life in razor-sharp fragments: as the farmer is more or less forced to give up his land, he recoups his loss by taking a sabbatical in Australia before returning to join the construction crew of the development, when he rejects the pressure of the building site and dreams of becoming a mountain guide, and ends up managing the small cafe run by his mother in the village. He is angry about and exhausted by all of the change; he hates the new pace and describes his life as parts of his intestines are being removed while still having to go on. In stark contrast, the second protagonist Egyptian 'sun-ray' and almost billionaire Samih Sawiris shows little signs of development. Every visit to the village is met with similar excitement of local press and praiseful bureaucrats. In press conferences he assures the inhabitants in spotless German about his courteous engagement. His language is carefully considered: trust,

Eero Saarinen,
John Deere World
Headquarters,
Moline,
Illinois,
1964

The corporate conquest
of the pastoral landscape
of the US.

Panel block housing,
Vladivostok,
Russia,
early 1960s

Synchronised smack planning
in earlier days: Soviet concrete
slabs cut mercilessly through
rugged terrain in Vladivostok.

stability, growth. He is charismatic, in his late 50s, neatly dressed in a *tenue de ville*, always a different checked shirt with the top-two buttons open. If you want, he could fit a Nutella commercial cliché. While at home in Egypt his country is falling apart, he is a bastion of peace and inner conviction to his Swiss development.

Although their faiths are ultimately interconnected, the two never meet in the movie, which might be the essence of the cliché of the dramatic effects of globalisation on the countryside: its subliminal message, despite its absent narrator, repeats the age-old narrative of the countryside's demise, leaving its inherent moralism purposefully unchallenged, therefore ignoring the root of the ambivalence (perhaps further induced by the format of the documentary). Is Andermatt a small village of indomitable Gauls holding out against (or at least dealing with) global-capital-driven invaders? It leaves unchallenged that Sawiris is free to invest his money in the way he sees fit. The farmer and his fellow villagers didn't consider finding more innovative ways of making more money and increasing their stability. But on the other hand, why was Sawiris not able to undertake something less ambitious and more inclined to the conditions of the village itself? Why a new Gstaad instead of a new Andermatt?

What strikes most is the laissez-faire attitude of practically all involved: the uneasy Godot-like complacency leading Sawiris to be both Devil and God to the villagers. Sawiris simultaneously seems only to be a caretaker/ executioner of the project's economically charged programme, fuelled by an overarching power from above – Adam Smith's 'invisible' hand uncloaking?

Camouflage

The laissez-faire mentality of both subjects in the film is undeniably reflected in the architecture of the large hotel resort. Where the Intourist hotels throughout the Soviet Union or the American corporate pastoralism of the 1950s and 1960s proposed a (partly Brutalist) conquest of the countryside, the chameleonic Chedi is its immediate opposite. Despite respectful intentions and Swiss ordinations it remains a programmatic Sisyphus labour: its scale and ambitions unavoidably form an oversized alien insertion in the village. Everything in the Chedi is according to the international template of good taste, comfort and leisure – including tablet-operated controls to cater for every need from your hotel bed. Promoted by the developer as 'living as in a glossy magazine', the interiors are sophisticated coffee-table books: colourful, warm and minimalistic/ Buddhist taste informs an almost dictatorial commitment to relaxation. It seems part of a collective decision – unconsciously made somewhere in

the 1980s – to transform a large portion of the world into a comfortable lounge with a cleanly bespoke Scandinavian modernity-inspired aesthetic – a successful version of Esperanto ruthlessly swallowing up all typologies from the sacral, to work, to the home.

The strain of leftover welfare ideals embraced by the market economy has failed to articulate the space outside of the lounge, hoping it wouldn't be necessary to do so. It is in this light that the Chedi's architectural modesty presents a serious issue that is painfully exposed in the documentary. Despite the project's positive effect on economy of the village, its architecture is deeply political: visitors are not residents, and residents are not visitors (despite a tragic double irony that both are part

*The more comfortable
the camouflaged
countryside becomes,
the more intense our
nostalgia.*

of the countryside looking for the same deal – finding inner peace). Its
sensitivities to local conditions remain incompatible with forms or rural
traditions like the backwardness of the mountain-crystal-cutting figure or
the farmer. Much of this culture has become irrelevant (at least for now),
consequently outsourced to heritage agencies acting as caretakers, or
lamented and mystified in countryside magazines like *Landlust* and *Homes
& Gardens*. Like in Andermatt, this radical opposition is hidden in versions
of the seemingly similar, shrewdly accelerating its master narrative of
demise and consequent lamenting and self-defeat: the more comfortable
the camouflaged countryside becomes, the more intense our nostalgia.
Willkommen in Andermatt. ⌂

Notes
1. TS Eliot, 'The Love Song of J
Alfred Prufrock', *Prufrock, and Other
Observations*, The Egoist (London), 1917.
2. Samih Sawiris in an interview 'The
A-Team', uploaded to YouTube in 2012:
https://youtu.be/7xF34mwJkoY.

Ambra Fabi and Giovanni Piovene

Durana, Albania
A Field of Possibilities

Durana is a disjointed metropolitan area that sprang up between Albania's two main cities Tirana and Durrës after the fall of communism. A government-run competition in late 2014 sought ideas for improvements to public space in the region. Here, **Ambra Fabi and Giovanni Piovene** of PIOVENEFABI – part of a multidisciplinary team that supplied one of the winning proposals – set out their vision, which works at multiple scales from masterplanning to individual architectural interventions.

'Durana' – literally the crasis of Tirana and Durrës – is a major metropolitan area that includes all of the territory between these two main Albanian cities (the capital and the main port) and is the economic heart of the whole country.

Commonly reduced to the thin strip of land bound to the Tirana-Durrës motorway, Durana is in reality a much more complex environment spanning the width of a valley. An evenly covered field, sloping gently from Tirana towards the Durrës coast, this inclined plane is contained to the south by hills, and defined by three important lines running from Tirana to the Adriatic Sea – a motorway, railway and the Tiranë River. The instant growth of this new city after the fall of the communist regime in 1991 resulted in a canvas of disconnected ecologies: the terraced hills, foothill villages, a linear city, industrial strip, the inhabited agricultural plain and the river shores. The sudden transition from a polarised territory characterised by a clear-cut division of the urban and the rural landscape, to a post-communist era laissez-faire drifting has caused the spillover of the regulated city from its borders and consequent invasion of many agricultural plots.

As a response to this context, at the end of 2014 the governmental agency Atelier Albania (established after the election of Edi Rama as Prime Minister) organised the Durana Competition. The declared scope of the competition, the brief for which was not assigned to any specific plot or programme, was more generally the improvement of the public space in the region: the generating of original and visionary interventions. The selected teams, two for each of the three sites into which the Durana region has been divided, had therefore to establish their own briefs for the pilot projects to be tested. The loose borders of the competition therefore represented a real opportunity to couple design and field research in the very compressed time span of three weeks.

The winning proposal for Lot 1 – the closest to Tirana – by the multidisciplinary team of PIOVENEFABI, YellowOffice, Stefano Graziani, Mobility in Chain, Archispace and Vladimir Myrtezai, deliberately considers the whole bandwidth of the valley – from the hills to the Tiranë River – and tackles multiple scales at once: an overarching vision at the territorial scale, an opportunity scan at the urban scale, and pilot projects at the architectural scale. With the goal of reconnecting ecologies, establishing hierarchies, repairing connections and reinforcing existing programmes, one of the main challenges of the project was the need to work systematically in an extremely fragmented context.

PIOVENEFABI and YellowOffice,
Lake Park,
Durana,
Albania,
2014

One of the three pilot projects of the Durana competition proposal is a park to be developed around a former water reservoir built under the communist regime. Strategically realised on the actual borders of the Greater Tirana area, it will stretch the idea of the city to its limits.

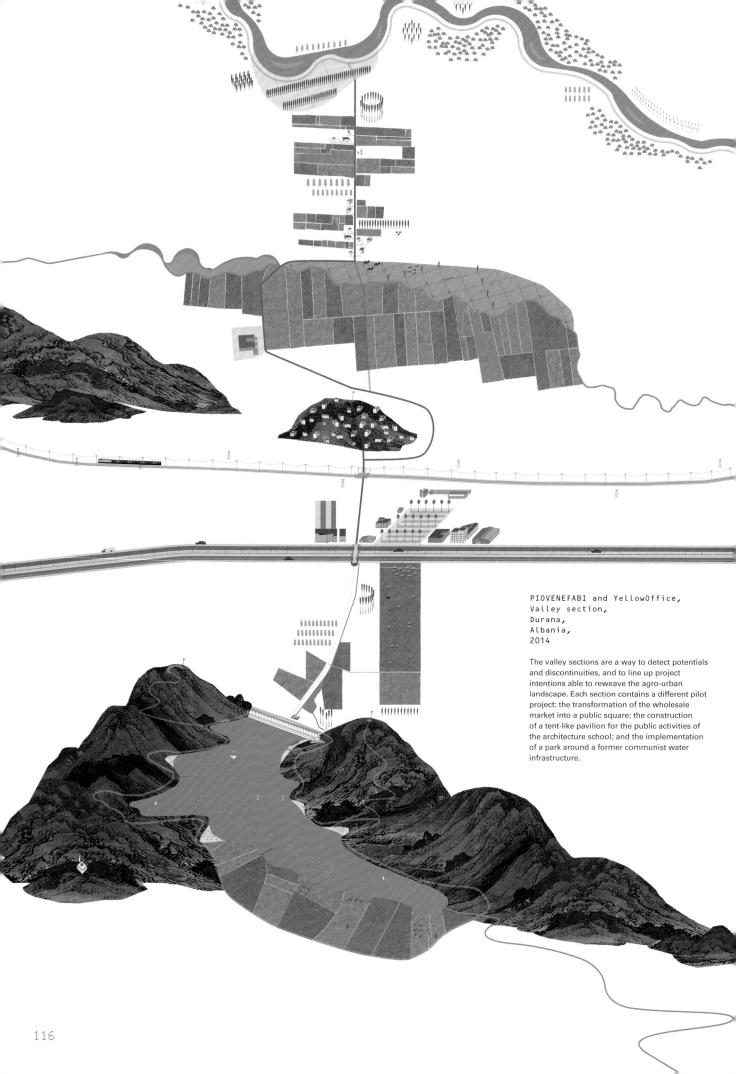

PIOVENEFABI and YellowOffice,
Valley section,
Durana,
Albania,
2014

The valley sections are a way to detect potentials
and discontinuities, and to line up project
intentions able to reweave the agro-urban
landscape. Each section contains a different pilot
project: the transformation of the wholesale
market into a public square; the construction
of a tent-like pavilion for the public activities of
the architecture school; and the implementation
of a park around a former communist water
infrastructure.

Three valley sections running from the artificial lakes to the Tiranë River present the opportunity to suggest a new direction of development. Through a series of punctual interventions on the existing fabric, such as access to small-scale public grounds, tracing new pedestrian routes, and reorienting pre-existing buildings and functions, the project aims to open up Durana's linear development into a loose urban entity able to preserve and foster its agro-urban nature instead of consuming it.

At the architectural scale, three pilot interventions are strongly bound to the context in a continuous effort to reinforce it: a market canopy as civic infrastructure, an open pavilion as a shared facility, and the lake as a playground – all sufficiently indeterminate to allow several uses.

Redefining the perimeter with the proposed market canopy will open up the existing wholesale market into a public square with 24-hour access, and reorientate the space towards an informal settlement that is currently completely cut off. The canopy will give shade to the small-scale informal vendors and also reorganise the public entrances to the market.

The tent-like pavilion, between the Polis University of Architecture and an important crossroads, will provide a covered open-air space, the programme for which is fully negotiable. On one side it will be a transition space between the scorching heat outside and the air-conditioned interior of the University building, allowing space for open-air classrooms and a cafeteria. On the other it will offer to the public a fully equipped event space.

The lake park – the most advanced of the three pilot projects with detailed design currently in progress – will transform an existing water reservoir into an agro-urban park with the simple addition of connecting roads and a few iconic architectural elements – a pier, a roof and a diving platform. This minimal intervention will turn a forgotten landscape at the border of Greater Tirana into a sports and recreational area while leaving the existing site unspoilt. The full realisation of the park, part of the new mayor's campaign, is keenly anticipated by the city, which has already begun organising mountain bike races and bike tours along the pathway that will soon become the park promenade. ᐁ

PIOVENEFABI and
YellowOffice,
Territorial Vision,
Durana,
Albania,
2014

The long-term vision for the whole valley includes the transformation of the expressway into a permeable urban road, and the outdated Tirana–Durrës line into a metropolitan light railway, and the development of a linear park along the shores of the Tiranë River.

This minimal intervention will turn a forgotten landscape at the border of Greater Tirana into a sports and recreational area while leaving the existing site unspoilt.

Durana as an evenly covered field,
Durana,
Albania,
2014

Since the fall of the communist regime in 1991, built areas have invaded rural plots, nevertheless following the irrigation pattern realised by Enver Hoxha's government. As a result, Durana is a mix of buildings and small-scale agriculture.

Neil Brenner

The Hinter

___

Urban

What defines the urban? And can the non-urban necessarily always be classified as rural? **Neil Brenner**, Director of the Urban Theory Lab at Harvard University Graduate School of Design, reflects on the lack of an overarching theory to describe these realms, and argues that what we call the countryside or the hinterland has become key to the process of capitalist urbanisation.

land, _ ised?

Desert agro-industrial
infrastructures,
Saudi Arabia,
2012

For several decades, subterranean water wells supported a highly mechanised, rationalised system of agro-industrial land-use in the desert landscape of Saudi Arabia. Today, the aquifers are depleted, and Saudi Arabia's role in global wheat production is rapidly declining.

The lecture (it might also be a scholarly article, a research report, a policy brief, a design proposal or a grant application) opens with a familiar reminder of an apparently unassailable fact, delivered from a trusted source: in 2007 (or was it 2003?), United Nations (UN) statisticians had determined that more than 50 per cent of the world's population was now living within cities. Although its lineages can be traced to efforts to decipher the accelerated industrialisation of capital in 19th-century Euro-America, the notion of an urbanising world has today become a ubiquitous interpretive frame.[1] Because the starting point of the lecture is so familiar, you ignore the author's framing gesture. Your thoughts drift as you wait for the real argument to begin – about the role of cities in current global transformations; and about the ongoing restructuring of cities. The presentation soon turns to these questions, and a debate ensues – about cities. These, everyone appears to agree, represent the elementary spatial units of the contemporary urban age. To what else could the concept of the urban possibly refer?

The Urbanisation *Problématique*

The notion of urbanisation has long been used in strikingly atheoretical ways, as if it were a purely descriptive, empirical basis for referencing a natural tendency of human spatial organisation. Within this framework, as Ross Exo Adams explains: 'Much like the weather, urbanisation is something that exists "out there", a condition far too "complex" to present itself as an object to be examined in its own right and thus something which can only be mapped, monitored compared and catalogued.'[2] This empiricist, naturalistic and quasi-environmental understanding of urbanisation persisted in various forms throughout the 20th century. In more recent decades, naturalistic models of urbanisation have acquired a powerful new lease of life in the science of 'big data', which tends to regard urban density as a condition that is basically akin to that of a closed biological system – subject to scientific laws, predictable and, thus, technically programmable.[3]

Contemporary UN declarations of a majority-urban world, and most major strands of mainstream global urban policy, planning and design discourse, likewise grasp the phenomenon of urbanisation via some version of this naturalistic, ahistorical and empiricist *dispositif*.[4] Here, urbanisation is assumed to entail the simultaneous growth and spatial diffusion of cities, conceived as generic, universally replicable types of human settlement. Thus understood, the contemporary urban age represents an aggregation of trends that have cumulatively increased the populations of urban centres. In this way, the urban-age metanarrative has come to serve as a framework not only of interpretation, but of *justification*, for a huge assortment of spatial interventions designed to promote what geographer Terry McGee has classically labelled 'city dominance'.[5] Around

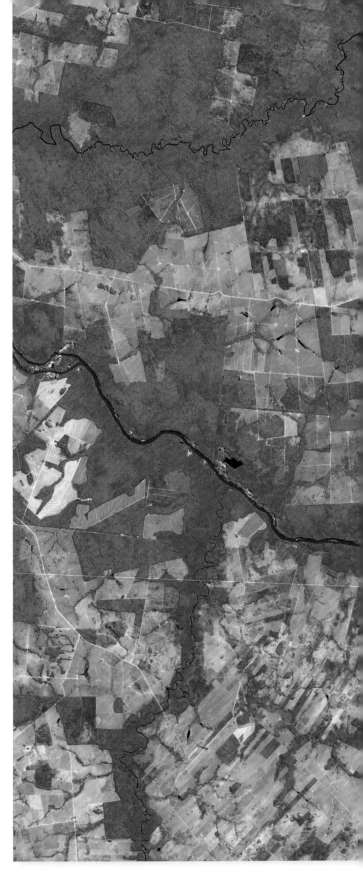

the world, the shared goal of such urbanisation strategies is building the 'hypertrophic city' – whether by densifying and extending extant megacity areas; by creating new urban settlement zones *ex nihilo* in pockets of the erstwhile countryside or along major transportation corridors; or by orchestrating rural-to-urban migration flows through a noxious cocktail of structural adjustment programmes, land grabbing, agro-industrial consolidation and ecological plunder.[6]

Deforestation,
Mato Grosso,
Brazil,
2006

Since the 1990s, major swathes of the Amazon have
been cleared to facilitate industrial agriculture
and expanded long-distance
logistics infrastructures.

The vision of urbanisation as 'city' growth is, however, anything but self-evident. On a basic empirical level, the limitations of the UN's census-based data on urbanisation are well known. The simple, but still apparently intractable, problem, to which sociologist Kingsley Davis already devoted extensive critical attention in the 1950s,[7] is that each national census bureau uses its own criteria for measuring urban conditions, leading to serious inconsistencies in comparative international data on urbanisation. In the current decade, for example, among those countries that demarcate urban settlement types based on a population size threshold (101 out of 232 UN member states), the criterion ranges from 200 to 50,000; no less than 23 countries opt for a threshold of 2,000, but 21 others specify the cutoff at 5,000.[8]

A host of comparability problems immediately follow, since 'urban' localities in one national jurisdiction may have little in common with those that are classified with the same label elsewhere. The use of various combinations of additional criteria in the other 131 member states – administrative, density based, infrastructural and socioeconomic – adds several further layers of confusion to an already exceedingly heterogeneous international data set. Should certain administrative areas automatically be classified as urban? What population density criterion, if any, is appropriate? Should levels of non-agricultural employment figure into the definition of urban areas (as they do in India, albeit only for male residents)? In short, even this brief glimpse into the UN's data tables reveals that the notion of a majority-urban world is hardly a self-evident fact. It is, rather, a statistical *artefact* constructed through a rather crude aggregation of national census data derived from inconsistent definitions of the phenomenon being measured.

The urban-age metanarrative has come to serve as a framework not only of interpretation, but of *justification*, for a huge assortment of spatial interventions

Interiorising the Constitutive Outside

Here arises a deeper theoretical problem with contemporary urban-age discourse. Even if the specificity of 'city' growth relative to other forms of demographic, socioeconomic and spatial restructuring could somehow be coherently delineated (for instance, through consistently applied, geospatially enhanced indicators for agglomeration), the question remains: How to delineate the process of urbanisation in *conceptual* terms?[9] Despite its pervasive representation as a neutral, generic background parameter within which spatial relations are situated, the process of urbanisation must itself be subjected to theoretical scrutiny. Doing so reveals at least two major epistemological fissures – logically unresolvable yet perpetually recurrent analytical problems – within the hegemonic *dispositif* of urban knowledge.

First, in the mainstream interpretive framework, urbanisation is said to entail the universal diffusion of 'cities' as the elementary units of human settlement. As is widely recognised, however, these supposedly universal units have assumed diverse morphological forms; they have been organised at a range of spatial scales; they have been mediated through a broad array of institutional, political, social, military and environmental forces; and they have been differentially articulated to their surrounding territories, landscapes and ecologies, as well as to other, more distant population centres. Given the *de facto* heterogeneity of agglomeration patterns, can a universal notion of 'the' city be maintained? And, if we do reject the hegemonic equation of cityness with singularity, must we not also abandon the vision of urbanisation as a universal process of spatial diffusion? Instead, heterogeneity, differentiation and variegation would have to be recognised, not simply

as unstructured empirical complexity, but as intrinsic, systemically produced properties of the urbanisation process itself.[10]

Second, in the hegemonic *dispositif*, urbanisation is defined as the growth of 'cities', which are in turn conceived as spatially bounded settlement units. This conceptual equation (urbanisation = city growth), coupled with the equally pervasive assumption of spatial boundedness, logically requires differentiating the city-like units in question from a putatively non-urban realm located outside them. However, the demarcation of a coherent urban/non-urban divide has proven thoroughly problematic, particularly since the accelerated worldwide industrialisation of capital in the 19th century. Indeed, within the mainstream urban *dispositif*, the delineation of a non-urban 'constitutive outside' is at once *necessary*, since it is only on this basis that cities' distinctiveness as such can be demarcated, and *impossible*, since (a) there are no standardised criteria for differentiating urban from non-urban settlement 'types', and (b) the apparent boundaries between urban settlements and their putatively non-urban exterior have constantly been exploded and rewoven at all spatial scales.

Despite the persistent naturalisation of ahistorical settlement typologies (urban, suburban, rural, wilderness) in mainstream geographical discourse, the relentless territorial extension of large centres of agglomeration into their surrounding fringes and peripheries was widely recognised by 20th-century planners and designers. Indeed, although it tends to be marginalised in canonical historical narratives, the process of urban territorial extension was arguably one of the formative concerns in relation to which the modern discipline of urban planning was consolidated. The field, in other words, has long contained a reflexively territorial

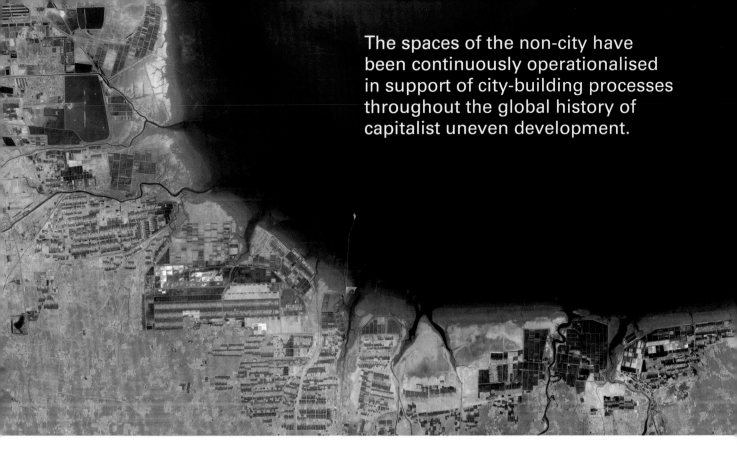

The spaces of the non-city have been continuously operationalised in support of city-building processes throughout the global history of capitalist uneven development.

Phosphate mining pits,
Central Florida,
1986

opposite:
Phosphate, an essential component of the fertiliser used in industrial agriculture, is mined through the construction of an extensively infrastructuralised regional landscape in which deposits can be extracted, processed and transported, generally with huge environmental impacts.

Urban-industrial infrastructures,
Bohai coast,
China,
2000

above:
As this image of salt production and shellfish farming infrastructures illustrates, the spatial fabric of industrial urbanisation involves the rationalisation of spatial organisation not only along coastlines, but across the fluid interface between land and ocean.

orientation, rather than being focused simply upon conditions within dense, bounded settlement units.[11]

Just as importantly, the developmental pathways of capitalist agglomerations have always been intimately intertwined with large-scale transformations of non-city spaces, often located at a considerable distance from the major centres of capital, labour and commerce. Mumford described this relation as an interplay between 'up-building' (vertical, horizontal and subterranean industrial-infrastructural clustering), and 'un-building' (*Abbau*), the degradation of surrounding landscapes through their intensifying role in supplying cities with fuel, materials, water and food, and in managing their waste products.[12] From the original dispossession of erstwhile rural populations through territorial enclosure to the intensification of land use, the construction of large-scale infrastructural investments and the progressive industrialisation of hinterland economies to support extraction, cultivation, production and circulation, the growth of the city has been directly facilitated through colossal, if unevenly developed industrial and environmental upheavals across the planet. In this sense, the rural, the countryside and the hinterland have never been reducible to a mere backstage 'ghost acreage' that supports the putatively front-stage operations of large population centres. Whatever their demographic composition, from the dense town networks of the Ganges Plain or Java to the barren wastelands of Siberia or the Gobi desert steppe, the spaces of the non-city have been continuously operationalised in support of city-building processes throughout the global history of capitalist uneven development. Such spaces are, therefore, as strategically central to the processes of creative destruction that

underpin the 'urbanisation of capital' as are the large, dense urban centres that have long monopolised the attention of urbanists.[13]

Faced with the relentless interplay between the up-building and un-building of spatial arrangements, along with the perpetual explosion of urban conditions across the variegated landscapes of global capitalism, can a settlement-based conception of urbanisation be maintained? Can the urban 'phenomenon' still be anchored exclusively within, and confined to, the city?[14] In fact, once the rigid analytical constraints imposed by such pointillist assumptions are relaxed, the static dualisms of mainstream urban theory (city/countryside, urban/rural, interior/exterior, society/nature) can be swiftly superseded. New analytical horizons thereby open: the geographies of urbanisation can be productively reconceptualised in ways that illuminate not only the variegated patterns and pathways of agglomeration, but the continuous production and transformation of an unevenly woven urban fabric across the many terrains of industrial activity (agriculture, extraction, forestry, logistics and tourism) that are today still being misclassified on the basis of inherited notions of the countryside, the rural, the hinterland and the wilderness.

Given the totalisations, blind spots and blind fields associated with the inherited *dispositif* of urban knowledge, perhaps an urban theory *without an outside* may be well-positioned to wrest open some productive new perspectives for both research and action on emergent landscapes of planetary urbanisation?[15]

Industrialised agriculture,
Minnesota,
2009

Through the widespread adoption of precision farming across the US Midwest, industrial planting, fertilisation and harvesting technologies have been customised to locational conditions at the scale of individual fields, rather than being applied uniformly across a farm or region.

The capitalist form of urbanisation continues to produce contextually specific patterns of agglomeration, but it also relentlessly transforms non-city spaces into zones of high-intensity, large-scale industrial infrastructure – *operational landscapes*.

Designing Other Urbanisations

The theoretical manoeuvres proposed here are intended not simply to permit the recognition of concrete, empirical complexity within, among and beyond urban centres, but as an epistemic basis for reconceptualising the essential properties of the process under investigation, and thereby for opening up new horizons for understanding and influencing contemporary urbanisation. As has been argued at length elsewhere, the epistemic fissures within contemporary urban discourse and practice can be transcended only through a radical break from the inherited urban *dispositif*, and from the one-sided vision of the urban condition that it anchors.[16] In any field of thought and action, new *dispositifs* of interpretation can only emerge when historical conditions destabilise inherited, doxic frameworks and engender an intensive search for an alternative basis for understanding and transforming the world. As evidenced in the recent escalation of epistemological debates among critically oriented urbanists, the field of urban theory presently appears to be in the throes of such a search.

Against this background, the current revival of interest in the rural, the countryside and the hinterland among many architects, landscape theorists and designers represents a salient, if still rather indeterminate development. Will such engagements simply entail a change of venue for the operations of design – a strategic shift 'back to the land' by architects in search of interesting new sites for their creative energies? Alternatively, might an architecturally grounded exploration of the world's non-city spaces help animate the project of developing new analyses, visualisations and designs of our emergent planetary urban fabric? Two concluding propositions may offer some orientation for such an endeavour.

First, inherited vocabularies for describing non-city spaces – rural, countryside, hinterland – are locked into an externalist framework that attempts to distinguish them, analytically and spatially, from the city. Today, however, we need new ways of interpreting and mapping the planet's variegated territories, landscapes and ecologies of urbanisation that are not opposed binaristically to the city, and that do not devalue their operational significance based upon a fetish of demographic criteria. The non-city is no longer exterior to the urban; it has become a strategically essential terrain of capitalist urbanisation.

Second, the capitalist form of urbanisation continues to produce contextually specific patterns of agglomeration, but it also relentlessly transforms non-city spaces into zones of high-intensity, large-scale industrial infrastructure – *operational landscapes*. In contrast to historically inherited hinterlands, in which various 'free gifts' of nature embedded in the land (materials, energy, labour, food, water) are appropriated to produce primary commodities, operational

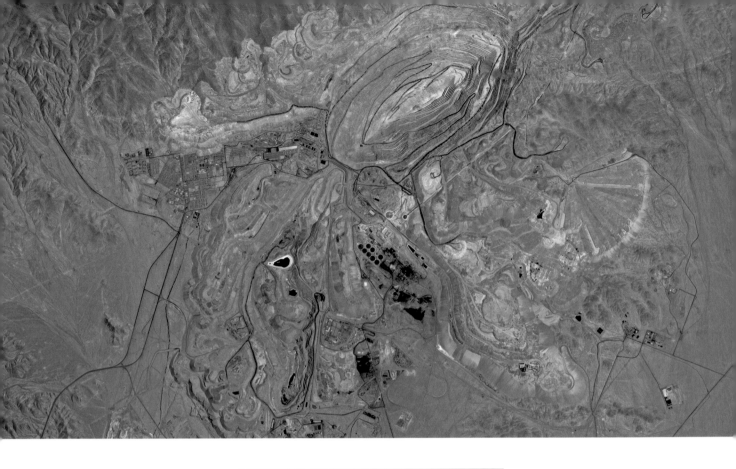

Chuquicamata copper mine, Northern Chile, 2016

All forms of industrial resource extraction, such as copper mining, entail the construction
of colossal, high-technology industrial infrastructures at the earth's surface and
underground to supply essential materials and minerals to the world's megacities.

landscapes involve the industrial redesign of agricultural, extractive and logistical activities to engineer the most optimal social, institutional, infrastructural, biological and ecological conditions for (generally export-oriented) capital accumulation. Whereas hinterlands merely 'host' primary commodity production within an inherited terrain, operational landscapes are consolidated through the active production of colossal urban-industrial spatial configurations that have been reflexively designed to accelerate and intensify the accumulation of capital on the world market.

The implications of these ideas for architectural and design interventions in the world's variegated non-city spaces remain to be elaborated. At minimum, they raise doubts about any approach that aspires to create fortified retreats or privatised enclaves (whether for ecosystem services, luxury consumption, private enjoyment or specialised industrial export activity) in the erstwhile countryside. Instead, they underscore the challenge of establishing politically negotiated, democratically coordinated, environmentally sane and socially meaningful modes of connectivity between the various places, regions, territories and ecologies upon which humans collectively depend for our common planetary life. As they mobilise their capacities to shape this emergent terrain

of intervention, designers confront an important ethical choice – to help produce maximally profitable operational landscapes for capital accumulation; or alternatively, to explore new ways of appropriating and reorganising the non-city geographies of urbanisation for collective uses and for the common good.

The perspective outlined here is oriented towards a counter-ideological project, one to which designers working in and on non-city terrains are particularly well positioned to contribute. How can we visualise, and thereby politicise, the encompassing but generally invisible webs of connection that link our urban way of life to the silent violence of accumulation by dispossession and environmental destruction in the world's hinterlands and operational landscapes? Insofar as designers bring distinctive forms of spatial intelligence and visualisation capacities to the sites in which they are engaged, they have an invaluable role to play in constructing new cognitive maps of the planet's unevenly woven urban fabric. Such maps may, in turn, provide much-needed orientation for all who aspire to redesign that fabric in more socially progressive, politically inclusive, egalitarian and ecological ways.

Insofar as these arguments challenge the dogma of the hypertrophic city – the prevalent assumption

Soya—bean production landscape, Cordoba Province, Argentina, 2016

Transnational corporations have expanded industrial soya-bean production in key agricultural regions of Argentina, contributing to an infrastructural standardisation of the landscape, as well as to a major public health crisis due to their use of agrochemicals.

that ever-larger cities represent humanity's inevitable future – they also open up a horizon for imagining a different form of urbanisation, an *alter*-urbanisation. Many urbanisations are, in fact, possible. Rather than being preordained through technological laws or economic necessity, urbanisation projects are collective political choices, a medium and product of power, imagination, struggle and experimentation. Can we imagine, for example, a form of urbanisation in which multiple settlement patterns and differentiated infrastructural arrangements are cultivated within a holistic framework of territorial development, balanced resource management and ecological stewardship? And can we envision a form of urbanisation in which households and communities that choose to remain rooted in less densely settled or remote zones will enjoy access to viable public infrastructures, sustainable livelihoods and some measure of political control over the basic conditions shaping their everyday lives? Perhaps the agency of design in the world's non-city spaces is precisely to facilitate the imagination and production of these and many other alter-urbanisations. ◹

Notes
1. Neil Brenner and Christian Schmid, 'The 'Urban Age' in Question', *International Journal of Urban and Regional Research*, 38 (3), 2014, pp 731–55. For the relevant UN data, see http://esa.un.org/unpd/wup/.
2. Ross Exo Adams, 'The Burden of the Present: On the Concept of Urbanisation', *Society and Space*, 11 February 2014: http://societyandspace.com/2014/02/11/ross-exo-adams-the-burden-of-the-present-on-the-concept-of-urbanisation/.
3. Brendan Gleeson, 'What Role for Social Science in the 'Urban Age'?', *International Journal of Urban and Regional Research*, 37 (5), 2013, pp 1839–51.
4. Brenner and Schmid, *op cit*.
5. Terry McGee, *The Urbanization Process in the Third World*, Bell & Sons (London), 1971.
6. Max Ajl, 'The Hypertrophic City Versus the Planet of Fields', in Neil Brenner (ed), *Implosions/Explosions: Towards a Study of Planetary Urbanization*, Jovis (Berlin), 2014, pp 533–50, and Mike Davis, *Planet of Slums*, Verso (London), 2006.
7. Kingsley Davis, 'The Origins and Growth of Urbanization in the World', *American Journal of Sociology*, 60 (5), 1955, pp 429–37.
8. Chandan Deuskar, 'What Does Urban Mean?', World Bank Sustainable Cities blog, 2 June 2015: http://blogs.worldbank.org/sustainablecities/what-does-urban-mean.
9. Neil Brenner and Christian Schmid, 'Towards a New Epistemology of the Urban', *CITY*, 19 (2–3), 2015, pp 151–82, and Neil Brenner, 'Theses on Urbanization', *Public Culture*, 25 (1), 2013, pp 86–114.
10. See Jenny Robinson, 'Cities in a World of Cities: the Comparative Gesture', *International Journal of Urban and Regional Research*, 51 (1), 2011, pp 1–23, and Ananya Roy, 'The 21st Century Metropolis: New Geographies of Theory', *Regional Studies*, 43 (6), 2009, pp 819–30.
11. See John Friedmann and Clyde Weaver, *Territory and Function*, University of California Press (Berkeley, CA), 1979. In contrast, Peter Hall's *Cities of Tomorrow*, Blackwell (Cambridge, MA), 2002, embodies a resolutely city-centric approach to urban planning history.
12. Lewis Mumford, *The City in History*, Harcourt, Brace and World (New York), 1961, pp 446–81.
13. David Harvey, *The Urbanization of Capital*, Johns Hopkins University Press (Baltimore, MD), 1985.
14. Henri Lefebvre, *The Urban Revolution*, trans R Bononno, University of Minnesota Press (Minneapolis, MN), 2003 (first published in 1970); and Brenner and Schmid, 'Towards a New Epistemology'.
15. Neil Brenner, 'Urban Theory Without an Outside', in *Implosions/Explosions, op cit*, pp 14–35.
16. Brenner and Schmid, 'Towards a New Epistemology, *op cit*.

Don't Waste Your Time in the Countryside

COUNTERPOINT 04/2016 No 242 AD

Patrik Schumacher

With the countryside becoming ever more sparsely populated as fewer people are needed to keep rural enterprises running, is there any point in engaging architects there? **Patrik Schumacher**, partner at Zaha Hadid Architects, argues that their time and skills are put to better use in cities, where buildings impact a far greater number of individuals and their social and cultural functionality is more important. Engineers, meanwhile, are perfectly equipped to devise generic solutions for the rural realm.

The bourgeoisie has subjected the country to the rule of the towns. It has created enormous cities, has greatly increased the urban population as compared with the rural, and has thus rescued a considerable part of the population from the idiocy of rural life.

— Karl Marx and Friedrich Engels, *The Communist Manifesto*, 1848[1]

Marx and Engels' assessment of the bourgeois city as an escape from rural idiocy should serve here as a reminder of two important points: that we should never forget the relative communicative poverty and cultural retardation of rural in comparison to urban life; and that we owe our prosperous and cultured urban civilisation to capitalism. My response to this issue of Δ and its basic thesis is ambivalent. On the one hand I share the issue's curiosity about the rural as a largely neglected zone for architectural engagement, and I am tempted, in the footsteps of Rem Koolhaas, to endorse this searching investigation into and probing of its potential via design projects. On the other hand, and especially since this issue has satisfied some of my curiosity about the contemporary countryside and offered a projective exploration of its potential, I remain highly sceptical about the pragmatic merit of this engagement. Indeed, I have come to the conclusion that neglecting the rural in favour of major urban centres (as primary or even exclusive arenas of our discipline's concern) reflects not so much a blind spot or prejudice of (always city-based) architects, but indeed justifiably registers the relative importance of these arenas and the relative urgency and value of their problematics in relation to architecture's core competency and thus in relation to its productive contribution to society. In short: my suspicion that Koolhaas's shift of interest from urban to rural conditions is a contrarian gesture rather than something to be emulated has been confirmed rather than assuaged.

Zaha Hadid
Architects,
Hyundai Corporate
Headquarters
competition, Seoul,
South Korea, 2015

below and next spread:
The aim of the proposal is maximal communicative capacity via the inter-visibility of all events. The built environment becomes a 360-degree interface of communication where the interior urbanism extends above, below and all around in layers – a massive investment merited by the productivity-enhancing synergies it facilitates.

Rural Architecture?

'Rural architecture' is an oxymoron. Architecture is an inherently urban discipline. Perhaps this thesis goes too far. However, it confirms my urban-focused work commitments and the positions I have promulgated elsewhere: the difference architecture can make in urban centres is much more momentous than what it might be able to do in rural conditions. This statement is especially pertinent in relation to the innovative frontier of the discipline where the skills and methodological sophistication of the most tooled-up protagonists continues to advance.

I am arguing here as an architect who regards not the logistical organisation of infrastructures, but the spatial, phenomenological and semiological ordering of social processes via architecture's communicative capacity as our primary societal task in the current specialisation of disciplinary competencies. Although all spaces of human communicative interaction – rural or urban – function via this ordering, it is the new density, dynamism, diversity and synergetic complexity of big cities that challenges us and urgently requires the most advanced design resources, and not the low density and simplicity of rural communicative situations that thus pose comparatively trivial architectural problems.

My thesis is that architects' attention to rural conditions is a relative waste of their precious time. Contemporary architecture is inherently urban. Even if this judgement is disputed, what is indisputable is that the number of people an architectural intervention affects is likely to be much lower in a rural context – a fact that is also reflected in construction budgets and real-estate values. This disadvantage of design investment in rural situations could only be compensated if very generic problems were identified and the solutions allowed for a massive generalised roll-out. But such projects are engineering led rather than architectural.

'Rural architecture' is an oxymoron.

Metropolitan Brain Versus Rural Muscle

My argument against shifting the discipline's attention from the urban to the rural is not an absolute and final position, but a pragmatic appraisal of relative productivity and value. Further, I believe that design investment in generic construction solutions for the rural landscapes of the world is much more likely to reside in the professional domain of engineers rather than architects, especially if we look further into the future. If we take the advanced industrialised and urbanised nations as guide – and so we should, for their superior productivity levels – we cannot fail to notice that the countryside is emptying, requiring fewer and fewer people to deliver more and more agricultural and mining productivity. It will therefore become a vast engineered landscape of physical machine-based production processes, where the absence or sparseness of human life will limit the need for architectural design.

All engineering design is process and machine design judged by criteria of technical functionality, whereas all architectural design is communication design judged by criteria of social functionality. In recent years, there have been huge advances in agricultural productivity: more produce is generated with less labour, land, water and fertilisers. And this has been achieved through research and development work in agro-science, genetic biology, geology, information processing and so on in the big cities. The metropolis is the brain of our civilisation. It is a communication hub and a social supercomputer. Most developmental bottlenecks are problems of communication. Material production takes place outside these centres, with fewer people directly involved in the physical production process. Human labour becomes mostly knowledge-based creative labour, networked into the super-brain that is the contemporary mega-metropolis directing the rural muscle. Leftist ideological criticism of the distinction and privileging of intellectual over manual labour is vain. This undeniable distinction is mirrored in the 'urban versus rural' distinction, and any attempt to 'unmask' it as ideological is equally vain.

Avant-Garde Versus Avant-Gardism

In their Introduction to this issue, the guest-editors talk about a 'discursive shift' from the urban to the rural, claiming 'the rural to be an emerging territory requiring as much innovation, strategic thinking and design experimentation as the city' (p 8). Really? Perhaps, but the required innovation is probably engineering rather than architectural. They observe that 'the vernacular that seemingly dominates the contemporary rural landscape' is reduced to 'generic concrete framed structures, driven by economic need and oblivious to any contextual factors' (p 8). This can lead us already to the conclusion that the value society places on architectural structures and architectural design work in rural areas does not merit a reversal of attention from the urban to the rural. The added value a man-month's worth of architectural design work can make with respect to rural design issues seems to be much lower than that which can be achieved by the same amount of design effort and competency in urban conditions: the marginal productivity of urban design trumps that of rural design.

The evidence of this is that work on most rural structures does indeed proceed without professional licensed architects, or if this is no longer a legal option in advanced countries, then at least without prominent (high-value) architects and thus without any recognition within the discipline's discourse. But, you may ask, is this not an artefact of a deficient discourse that is finally being remedied here? Well, that is indeed the hypothesis of this 𝝙.

The metropolis is the brain of our civilisation. It is a communication hub and a social supercomputer.

131

However, it is a hypothesis that comes from architects, without any signals as to demand from the prospective clientele. Even if we do not necessarily take the market signals as decisive indicators and accept that the discourse leads the discipline (as my theory of architectural autopoiesis posits),[2] the discipline cannot diverge for too long from social and economic realities and societal valuations (as expressed via market demand) without losing credibility and missing its societal function. While an avant-garde initiative that counter-poses current realities with new possibilities is not inherently unviable, like every speculative venture it is a risky investment. Risks have to be taken by all explorations, however is such investment in rural possibilities promising enough? I doubt it, because there are no real clients calling for this work.

In general, there is an especially risky entrepreneurial element in avant-garde discourses that venture beyond the scope of finding new spatial/architectural solutions to problems posited by clients and instead try to identify new problems and new briefs as the basis for architectural innovations, substituting themselves for the missing clients. This approach (which seems prevalent in this issue of ⌂) multiplies uncertainty. The method is doubly speculative: on the side of the presumed problems as well as the proposed solutions. The prospect that this avant-gardism might become a true avant-garde is therefore accordingly improbable. An avant-garde will be validated and confirmed as such only in retrospect, only if its anticipations turn out to become spearheads of eventual mainstream professional practice creating economic value for real clients with effective purchasing power. My appraisal of the 'rural turn' is therefore very sceptical: the proposition is too improbable to merit its hype.

Markets Versus Anti-Capitalist Moralising

The spirit of the guest-editors, of most articles in this issue, and of the projects they refer to is guided by the seemingly laudable intention to identify and invest in the supposedly neglected, forgotten rural victims of political and economic processes of urbanisation. There is a moralising element here that we should be very cautious about. What worries me in particular is the pervasive anti-capitalist bias that permeates most accounts and arguments here.

The guest-editors lament that an 'increasing number of sites become disconnected or disrupted through infrastructural development' and that 'macro-infrastructure prioritises the co-option of rural territory for urban processes' (p 9). In principle we should acknowledge that these priorities most probably reflect the economic value hierarchies of the society concerned and are thus an inevitable part of any economical land utilisation. In capitalist contexts these priorities are established via markets involving all potentially concerned parties in bidding and negotiation processes to establish the most productive way of balancing costs and benefits. In the context of China, and in general where land resources and infrastructure projects are government controlled rather than resulting from market processes, questions about the use of political power can and should indeed be asked. But 'critical' analysis should no longer proceed from an implicit, taken-for-granted left/socialist perspective. This kind of routine, presumptive 'critical' reasoning no longer has any intellectual credibility.

What strikes me as most problematic in the 'critical' discourse of this 𝐃 – and this I think is intrinsically connected with the strong anti-capitalist priors – is its barrenness with respect to constructive proposals and indeed the absence of any actionable conclusions. Neil Brenner's article is the most questionable in this respect. He denounces urbanisation processes as 'orchestrating rural-to-urban migration flows through a noxious cocktail of structural adjustment programmes, land grabbing, agro-industrial consolidation and ecological plunder' (p 121). Whether land is 'grabbed', purchased or politically allocated, the primary question is what its most productive and prosperity-enhancing use would be.

Notes

1. Karl Marx and Friedrich Engels, *The Communist Manifesto* [1848], HarperCollins (Toronto), e-publication, 2014, p 5.
2. Patrik Schumacher, *The Autopoiesis of Architecture, Vol I: A New Framework for Architecture*, John Wiley & Sons (Chichester), 2011.
3. See FA Hayek, 'The Use of Knowledge in Society', *American Economic Review*, XXXV (4), September 1945, pp 519–30, and FA Hayek, 'Competition as a Discovery Procedure', *New Studies in Philosophy, Politics, Economics and the History of Ideas*, Routledge and Kegan Paul (London), 1978.

It is my contention (and political economy hypothesis) that a market process with minimal political interference and thus maximal freedom of exchange for the exploration of value potentials is our collective best bet for utilising all relevant knowledge to discover and realise the best land-use opportunities.[3] Brenner proclaims that 'designers confront an important ethical choice – to help produce maximally profitable operational landscapes for capital accumulation; or alternatively, to explore new ways of appropriating and reorganising the non-city geographies of urbanisation for collective uses and for the common good' (p 126). But ethical choices without economic understanding are blind. And taking the opposition of profitability and the common good for granted is intellectually bankrupt. Rather the inverse should be the default assumption: markets confirm social merit via profitability. The formula of collective appropriation for the common good was always too abstract to guide concrete action, but since the collapse of communism it is altogether empty. 𝐃

CONTRIBUTORS

Anders Abraham is Professor and Head of the Master's programme in Art and Architecture at the Royal Danish Academy of Fine Arts School of Architecture. He runs the Copenhagen-based Anders Abraham Architects. He was educated at the Cooper Union in New York, and Cranbrook Academy of Art in Michigan. His work has been shown in numerous exhibitions, for example at the Danish Architecture Centre, Norwegian Centre for Design and Architecture, and the Venice Architecture Biennale. A new edition of his book *A New Nature* has recently been launched by Lars Müller Publishers.

Neil Brenner is Professor of Urban Theory and Director of the Urban Theory Lab at the Harvard University Graduate School of Design (GSD). His writing and teaching focus on critical urban theory, geopolitical economy and capitalist urbanisation. He is the editor of *Implosions/Explosions: Towards a Study of Planetary Urbanization* (Jovis, 2014) and the author of *New State Spaces: Urban Governance and the Rescaling of Statehood* (Oxford University Press, 2004). Two new books, *Critique of Urbanization* (Bauwelt Fundamente Series, Birkhäuser) and *New Urban Spaces: Urban Theory and the Scale Question* (Oxford University Press) are forthcoming in 2016.

Christina Capetillo is a Danish architect and photographer. She is Associate Professor and Co-Head of the Master's programme in Landscape Art at the Royal Danish Academy of Fine Arts School of Architecture. In her photographic works and artistic research she focuses on the contemporary landscape as a cultural condition. Recent exhibitions include 'Land Records', 'Outside the Rush' and 'Landworks'. Her work is represented in the collections of Museum für Photographie in Braunschweig, the Brandts Museum, Skagens Museum and Ny Carlsberg Foundation. In 2015 she was awarded the Eckersberg Medal for her contribution to Danish photography.

Ambra Fabi studied at the Accademia di Architettura di Mendrisio and at the École Nationale Supérieure d'Architecture (ENSA) Paris-Belleville. From 2007 to 2010 she worked as art director and project leader at Architekturbüro Peter Zumthor und Partner, Haldenstein, and from 2010 to 2012 in her own office in Milan. In 2013 she founded with Giovanni Piovene the office PIOVENEFABI. Since 2010 she has also been working at the Accademia di Architettura di Mendrisio with Freek Persyn (51N4E), Éric Lapierre and Bijoy Jain (Studio Mumbai). She has been a teaching professor at IED Cagliari and lectured in Antwerp, Tirana, Munich and Aachen.

Rainer Hehl is an architect/urban planner and currently professor at the Technical University Berlin and at the Yokohama National University, Institute for Advanced Sciences. He directed the Master's of Advanced Studies in Urban Design at ETH Zurich, conducting research and design projects on urban developments in emerging territories with a focus on Brazil. He holds a PhD on urbanisation strategies for informal settlements from ETH Zurich, investigating case studies in Rio de Janeiro. In addition to having lectured widely on urban informality, popular architecture and hybrid urbanities, he co-founded the BAÚ Collaborative urban design office.

Charlotte Malterre-Barthes is an architect and urban designer. She is Director of Studies of the Master of Advanced Studies in Urban Design programme at ETH Zurich, investigating the urban dynamics of Cairo, and is currently working on her doctoral degree on food and territories, a case study of Egypt. She co-founded the urban research office OMNIBUS. She studied at the ENSA Marseille, TU Vienna and ETH Zurich, and has worked in India with Balkrishna Doshi. She has lectured and taught workshops at the Architectural Association (AA) in London, at the Architectural Foundation, Storefront for Art and Architecture, University of Hong Kong and FCL-Singapore. Her work has been published in various magazines.

Sandra Parvu is an architect and a faculty member at the ENSA Paris-Val de Seine. She has published *Grands ensembles en situation: Journal de bord de quatre chantiers* (Metispresses, 2011) as well as articles in European architecture and landscape magazines such as *Urbanisme*, *Faces*, *Candide*, *OASE* and the *Journal of Landscape Architecture*. She holds a PhD from the École des Hautes Études en Sciences Sociales in Paris, and was educated at the University of Cambridge and Princeton University.

Stephan Petermann holds a Master's degree in the History of Architecture and the Theory of Building Preservation from the University of Utrecht (2001–07) and studied architecture at the Technical University of Eindhoven (2001–05). He joined OMA in 2006, assisting OMA's founder Rem Koolhaas with lectures, texts and research. He was one of the associates in charge of Koolhaas's 'Fundamentals' Venice Architecture Biennale in 2014. He is currently preparing two AMO research projects: one about the metabolism of workspaces, the other on the future of the countryside in collaboration with the Harvard GSD.

Giovanni Piovene studied at Università IUAV di Venezia and at the ENSA Paris-Belleville. After working for the Shrinking Cities Office in Berlin, he co-founded the Salottobuono office in 2007. In 2013 he co-founded PIOVENEFABI with Ambra Fabi. He is also the founder and editor of the architecture magazine *San Rocco*. He has taught at the IUAV and ISIA Urbino, and assisted at the Accademia di Architettura di Mendrisio. He is currently working at the École Polytechnique Fédérale de Lausanne. He has lectured at the IUAV, Polytechnic University of Milan, Accademia di Architettura di Mendrisio and Escuela Superior de Arquitectura (ESARQ) in Barcelona.

Cole Roskam is Assistant Professor of Architectural History in the Department of Architecture at the University of Hong Kong. He holds Master's and doctoral degrees in art and architectural history from Harvard University. His research examines architecture's role in mediating moments of transnational interaction and exchange between China and other parts of the world. His articles and essays have appeared in *Architectural History*, *Artforum International*, *Grey Room*, the *Journal of Architectural Education* and the *Journal of the Society of Architectural Historians*, among others.

Patrik Schumacher is partner at Zaha Hadid Architects (ZHA). He joined Zaha Hadid in 1988 and has been seminal in developing ZHA to become a 400-strong global architecture and design brand. In 1996 he founded the Design Research Laboratory at the AA where he continues to teach. He lectures worldwide and recently held the John Portman Chair in Architecture at Harvard's GSD. In 2008 he coined the term 'Parametricism' and has since published a series of manifestos promoting Parametricism as the new epochal style for the 21st century.

David Grahame Shane trained at the AA in London and at Cornell University in New York (PhD). He teaches Graduate Urban Design at Columbia University and is a Visiting Professor at the Polytechnic University of Milan, also participating in masterclasses at the University of Venice. He has lectured widely and published in architectural journals in Europe, the US and Asia. He is the author of *Recombinant Urbanism: Conceptual Modelling in Architecture, Urban Design and City Theory* (John Wiley & Sons, 2005) and *Urban Design Since 1945: A Global Perspective* (John Wiley & Sons, 2011). He guest-edited, with Brian McGrath, the △ title *Sensing the 21st-Century City: Close-Up and Remote* (November 2005).

Sheng-Yuan Huang is the principal of Fieldoffice Architects in Yilan, Taiwan, and holds a Master's degree in architecture from Yale University. He worked for Eric Owen Moss Architects as a Project Associate before returning to Taiwan, and also taught at North Carolina State University.

Deane Simpson is an architect and urbanist. He is associate professor at the Royal Danish Academy of Fine Arts School of Architecture where he leads the Urbanism and Societal Change Master's programme. He was previously a unit master at the AA in London, a professor at the Bergen School of Architecture (BAS), and an associate at Diller + Scofidio in New York. He received his Master's from Columbia University in New York and doctorate from the ETH Zurich. His most recent book, *Young-Old: Urban Utopias of an Aging Society*, was released by Lars Müller Publishers in 2015.

Milica Topalovic is an architect and urbanist, researching urban territories and urbanisation processes. She is an Assistant Professor of Architecture and Territorial Planning at ETH Zurich. From 2011 to 2015 she studied the relationship between the city state and its hinterlands at the ETH Future Cities Laboratory in Singapore. She graduated with distinction from the Faculty of Architecture in Belgrade, received her Master's degree from the Dutch Berlage Institute, and was Head of Research at the ETH Studio Basel. She is a co-author of *Belgrade: Formal/Informal* (Scheidegger & Spiess, 2012) and *Constructed Land – Singapore 1924–2012* (ETH Zurich, 2014) and is currently also conducting a research project on the European countryside.

Sandeep Virmani is an environmentalist and architect. Based in the desert of Kutch in Sindh, western India, he has worked on issues of water management to ensure communities are self-reliant on their local aquifers and recycle wastewater; with pastorals to conserve their grasslands and breeds as an example of frugality and simple living; has helped farmers conserve their crop biodiversity to deal with assured production, even in the face of climate change; and organised communities and artisans to build sustainably with earth, wood, bamboo, stone and recycle both industry and construction waste for buildings. He has recently begun organising communities to save and conserve the rare and endangered flora and fauna in their villages.

Yu-Hsiang Hung is a project architect and currently also the academic affairs coordinator at Fieldoffice Architects. He received his MPhil in Architecture and Urban Design from the AA Projective Cities in London in 2015.

What is *Architectural Design*?

Founded in 1930, *Architectural Design* (⌀) is an influential and prestigious publication. It combines the currency and topicality of a newsstand journal with the rigour and production qualities of a book. With an almost unrivalled reputation worldwide, it is consistently at the forefront of cultural thought and design.

Each title of ⌀ is edited by an invited Guest-Editor, who is an international expert in the field. Renowned for being at the leading edge of design and new technologies, ⌀ also covers themes as diverse as architectural history, the environment, interior design, landscape architecture and urban design.

Provocative and inspirational, ⌀ inspires theoretical, creative and technological advances. It questions the outcome of technical innovations as well as the far-reaching social, cultural and environmental challenges that present themselves today.

For further information on ⌀, subscriptions and purchasing single issues see:

www.architectural-design-magazine.com

Volume 85 No 4
ISBN 978 1118 914830

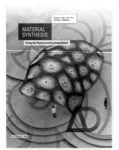

Volume 85 No 5
ISBN 978 1118 878378

Volume 85 No 6
ISBN 978 1118 915646

Volume 86 No 1
ISBN 978 1118 910641

Volume 86 No 2
ISBN 978 1118 736166

Volume 86 No 3
ISBN 978 1118 972465